The Baby Loss Guide

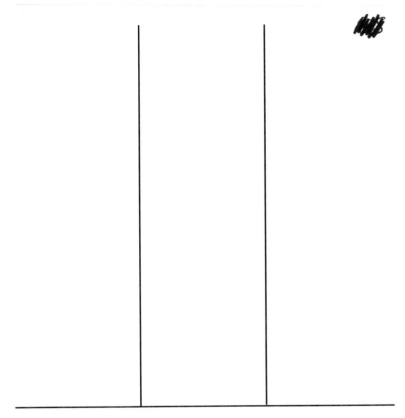

Richmond upon Thames Libraries

Renew online at www.richmond.gov.uk/libraries

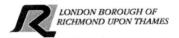

LONDON BOROUGH OF
RICHMOND UPON THAMES

The Baby Loss Guide

Practical and compassionate support
with a day-by-day resource to navigate
the path of grief

ZOË CLARK-COATES

S

First published in Great Britain in 2019 by Orion Spring
an imprint of The Orion Publishing Group Ltd
Carmelite House, 50 Victoria Embankment
London EC4Y 0DZ

An Hachette UK Company

1 3 5 7 9 10 8 6 4 2

Every effort has been made to ensure that the information in the book
is accurate. The information in this book may not be applicable in each
individual case so it is advised that professional medical advice is obtained
for specific health matters and before changing any medication or dosage.
Neither the publisher nor author accepts any legal responsibility for any
personal injury or other damage or loss arising from the use of the
information in this book. In addition, if you are concerned about
your diet or exercise regime and wish to change them, you
should consult a health practitioner first.

A CIP catalogue record for this book is
available from the British Library.

ISBN (Trade paperback) 978 1 4091 8543 7
ISBN (eBook) 978 1 4091 8546 8

Contents

PART 2: 60 DAYS OF SUPPORT AND JOURNALLING

Introduction

The *Baby Loss Guide* deals with a huge subject and I am sure many of you have opened up this book to see what the pages might contain. My personal experience with baby loss means I know what it's like to feel desperate and how those feelings can make you seek out every book available to man – and woman – in the hope that it can rescue you from pain. Let me tell you at the start: however helpful (I hope) this book may be to you on your journey, it won't save you from the agony you are experiencing if you are grieving. Oh, how I wish it could; that is what I wanted when I went looking for self-help books, and I long to be able to give you that – but nothing like that exists in the world. There is no fast pass through grief – it has to be felt and lived – so please read this book with that in mind. This isn't a lifeboat sent to drag you out of the water; it's a friend with a lifering hoping to make you feel less alone, and a guide to navigate the rough seas ahead.

I could have written a clinical book full of medical

information and facts, of which there are many. But that is the last thing I personally would have wanted to read after losing my babies. While I was in a fog of grief, any information I did read blindsided me with terminology I often didn't understand and facts that left me feeling cold and scared.

This made me think: what did I want? More importantly perhaps, what did I need post-loss? The answer to those questions was vital, as I knew this book needed to deliver that.

Yes, I did want some basic medical information on loss, not just the losses I had encountered, but also other types of baby loss. This new world I now walked in showed me there was more to baby loss than I had ever thought. There were different types of loss, varying medical and non-medical treatments and various physical responses and emotional reactions – so I knew I needed to include this detail. For some this information may be vital, for others it may not be needed at all, but it may broaden your knowledge about loss, which could be helpful to you or useful when supporting someone through loss.

My world post-loss felt so scary and I was given very few answers, which meant I lived in a real state of uncertainty. I had hundreds of questions, and to have had just a few of these answered, or at least discussed openly, would have helped. So, I have chosen to include some topics in this book that are rarely discussed in the public domain, such as trying again post-loss, intimacy post-loss and post-loss fear.

I also needed something that helped to explain my walk through grief to others, as at the time of suffering with repeated loss I could not find the words. When you are bereft, the last thing you feel able to do is educate those around you on the grieving process, so if I'd had a book I could have given to family and friends it would have been the ultimate gift, for them and me.

I needed day-by-day support – a companion, if you like, to walk with me through grief. Following the release of my first book, *Saying Goodbye*, a huge number of people told me the daily support section saved them from feeling lost and alone, so it was an easy decision to include one in *The Baby Loss Guide*. This time, I wanted to include a journal section as part of the book, so it can become a personal diary for you. Some may fill it in and never look back at what they wrote, while others may find it comforting to look back on their walk through grief and see how far they have journeyed. I encourage you to make this space your own and to use it to creatively express your pain and your feelings, as the simple act of writing down your thoughts can help process them.

Finally, I wanted a book that gave me hope. I have walked in that dark place, that black hole that feels lacking in love and devoid of grace. That is why, on leaving that horrid grief-filled room, I left a light on, by setting up the charity. And now I want this book to be a light to those who need it. I want people to see it as their torch, and by utilising the light it gives, I hope it will help them find a path out of the darkness. This is why I have not just included my views and experiences on loss, I have also included others' stories. Grief is unique to every person, therefore every person would describe it differently; but there are common feelings and emotions, and I hope by hearing from many different people you will read things that resonate with you, and in turn this will make you feel less alone.

So, yes, I set myself a big task . . .

Am I daunted? Of course.

But if my words help you even in a small way, I will be happy. If they help you a lot, I will be overjoyed.

Please come and find me on social media; I love to hear from readers and I want to hear your stories.

Much love

Zoë x

Instagram - @Zoeadelle

Twitter - @ClarkCoates

Facebook - @ZoeAdelleCC

Pinterest - /zoeclarkcoates/

Website – www.zoeadelle.co.uk

My Story in Brief

I put off having children, having watched a close friend go through the horrendous experience of miscarriage. I didn't know how I would personally cope with such a loss. However, once I had been married for over 12 years to my soulmate (we married young), setting up a successful business, suddenly my biological clock started ticking. Yes, I too thought this was an urban myth – that one day you could be satisfied with no children, then the next you have a burning desire to reproduce, but it happened to me.

After a while, I started having symptoms that showed me I was pregnant, but very sadly it ended in a miscarriage, and my way of coping was to pretend it hadn't happened. I didn't want to be one of those statistics which state that up to one in four pregnancies end in miscarriage, and surely if I didn't acknowledge it, it didn't really happen. I pushed all emotion down and we went into total denial. We later named this baby Cobi.

Within a couple of months, we were blessed with another

pregnancy. We decided to keep it a secret from the family, and to tell them at Christmas, as we knew they would be surprised. There seems to be a presumption in society that if you are going to have children it will happen in the first three years of a relationship, and if there aren't signs of tiny pattering feet by then, the assumption is it's just not going to happen.

We went for our first scan, and we had a heart-stopping moment when the sonographer said, 'Are you sure you have your dates right, as I can't see anything?' Following our assurance that the dates were indeed correct, she suddenly announced, 'Oh, there it is', and on the screen we witnessed the miracle of life, our tiny little baby, wriggling around, with its little heartbeat fluttering away. We were, of course, over the moon. She did mention that she could see a pool of blood in the womb, and warned me I should expect a little blood loss at some point, but not to worry about it at all. That evening I did get a little spotting, and if I'm honest I did panic. Any woman will tell you, if you see any signs of blood while pregnant, this fear just swells from nowhere. But by the following day the spotting had stopped, so peace returned.

A while later I caught the flu, and was bedridden for a week. Then as quickly as it had stopped, the bleeding started again, but this time it felt different. We found a clinic that agreed to scan me. After an age, we were called into the scanning room, and the doctor immediately activated the all-telling machine. There, on the screen, we saw our baby for the second time – kicking away, showing no signs of distress or concern . . . what a relief!

We were due to go to a party on the Saturday evening, so, figuring that resting up might stop any further bleeding,

I stayed in bed during the day, constantly doing that maternal stroke of the stomach, which somehow feels like you're comforting and caring for your child within. But when I got up that evening, I felt a sudden rush of blood, and I knew my baby had just died. I lay on the floor begging God to save her, crying out to the only One who truly controls life and death, but I knew deep down it was in vain. I knew she was destined to be born into heaven not onto earth. Mother's instinct? Who knows, but I knew her little heart was no longer beating within her or me.

We rushed to A&E where I was sadly met with little concern; I was even asked if it was an IVF baby as I was so upset. 'Why?' I asked. 'Is it not normal to cry over a naturally conceived child?' They had no answer. They didn't examine me, I was just told, 'There is nothing we can do, let nature take its course, what will be will be.' I was given an appointment for an emergency scan in a week's time and told to go home to bed.

The next day, the bleeding slowed down, and we left messages on numerous clinic answering machines begging for an appointment as soon as possible. The following morning, we got a call from a wonderful clinic telling us to come over and they would scan me. It was to be one of the longest journeys of my life.

We were called from the waiting area, and into a small room. I was told to get on the bed, and the scanner was booted up. After what seemed like an eternity of silence, I finally willed up the courage to ask, 'Can you see the baby? Is it all okay?' I didn't really need to ask, my baby was still, the only movement on the screen came from my body, not hers. My question was met with the worst answer: 'Zoë, I'm sorry to say there isn't a heartbeat.' I screamed and then pleaded for a second scan, which the midwife did. She then went to get a consultant; he came in shaking his head, saying the same words, ones that would become very familiar to us over the coming months: 'I'm so sorry.' We were quickly put in a tiny room, where we sobbed, wailed, and clung to each other; we phoned our family and, on hearing the words coming out of our own mouths, the nightmare of our reality dawned on us: our baby had died, she was still here with us, but we would never hold her hand, or rock her to sleep. 'What now?' we asked. We were told we could go the surgical route or the natural route. I chose the natural route, as the thought of going to a hospital where my baby would be just extracted from me seemed wrong; it was my baby, and I wanted to keep her with me for as long as possible.

What I wasn't prepared for was that the ordeal would go on for a week. A scan after a few days showed the baby had grown further, which is apparently totally normal, as the blood supply is still making the baby grow, but her heart remained still, no spark of life was seen . . . and, 'No, Zoë, sadly your baby hasn't miraculously come back to life. Yes, we know you had hoped it would happen.'

Was I wrong to hope this may be the case? That if I prayed non-stop, if I kept rubbing my stomach night and day, somehow her heart would just start up again. I had been told by a nurse that there was one case of it somewhere in the world once, so was I misguided to believe I could be the second?

We returned home and the days passed, long and slow. Someone asked me how I could allow a dead baby to stay inside me. 'Because it's my baby,' I said. Why anyone would presume that her death made her any less precious, or me any less loving, I'm not sure, but for some carrying a dead baby within is creepy, morbid and wrong. To me I was being her mother, keeping her safe in the place that had become her haven. I felt she was entitled to remain there until she decided to leave; it wasn't my place to suddenly evict her, and I was prepared to wait as long as needed for her to dictate the timing of our meeting.

A week to the day after her heartbeat stopped, labour started, and within 24 hours I had delivered my child, my daughter, Darcey.

For the next six weeks, my body raged with pregnancy hormones as it wrongly assumed I was still carrying a child. All day and night, sickness continued, along with the indigestion and headaches. What were once reassuring symbols of pregnancy were now horrendous reminders of what was no more. The oddest thing then started to occur, almost on a daily basis – complete strangers would randomly ask me if I had children. Each time it was like I was being thumped in the stomach. I instantly faced a dilemma: whether to protect the feelings of the person who had just asked me this very innocent question, and simply say, 'No, I haven't', but, by doing so, I would be denying my child's existence; or bravely say, 'I have actually, but they died.' I tried both, and both felt wrong, and I quickly learnt I was in a lose–lose situation, and I should just do whatever felt right at the time.

I was met with lots of well-meaning statements like 'Well, at least it proves you can conceive' and 'Sometimes the womb just needs practice'. Thankfully, the less sensitive comments were in a minority, as I was blessed to have my husband – my hero – by my side, not always knowing what to say, but being wise enough to know that words often aren't needed, and that just to hold me would mostly be enough. And then there were my parents, who sat with us and filled endless buckets with their own tears, while helping to empty ours. The rest of our family and friends were amazing, their support was tangible, and though most had no comprehension of what we were experiencing, they just made it clear to us that they were there, and that meant the world to us.

Some may think this extinguished the biological clock, but it didn't; it only increased my desire to have a baby, though the fear that I would never become a mum was overwhelming.

Two months later, I tragically lost my third baby (Bailey) via a miscarriage. We kept this to ourselves, as we felt the family had gone through enough, and they were under the impression we had only ever lost one baby, so to tell them about this loss would lead us to admitting to them, and to ourselves, that this in fact was our third child to grace the heavenly gates.

Then we got pregnant again, and following a frightening nine months, where we had fortnightly scans, we were finally handed our beautiful daughter, Esme Emilia Promise, weighing 6lb 15oz. The relief was profound, and there are no words to explain the elation of finally getting to hold and protect my tiny little girl.

We loved being parents so much; the thought of having another child was mentioned when she was one and a half, even though we had declared to all and sundry that we would be stopping at one! Nothing had prepared us for the amount of joy a little one can add to your life; there was nothing about being a mum I didn't love, so we decided to try for a brother or sister for Esme.

Naïvely, having given birth to a healthy, thriving child who went to full term, we believed our dealings with miscarriage and loss were in the past, and any further pregnancies would resemble that of our last one, rather than our first three. We were wrong.

We got pregnant, and all the initial scans were perfect, then on one of our appointments the scan showed our baby's heartbeat had simply stopped (again). Time went into slow motion when we were told, I literally couldn't speak. I wasn't prepared to tumble through that hidden trap door, from expectant mother to missed miscarriage, a fourth time. I misguidedly thought to lose a child when you already have one would hurt less, but I was wrong. It is different but not less. You aren't grieving the fact that you may never be a mother to a living child (as you are already), but it hurts in lots of new ways – we were constantly asking ourselves whether this baby would have laughed in the same way as our little girl. Would they have talked in the same way? The grief was all-consuming and I felt like I had been pushed off a cliff edge with no warning. We named our baby Samuel.

In a bid to try to protect our little girl from seeing any upset, I only allowed myself to cry in private and forced myself to keep things as normal as possible for her, but this was an Everest-type challenge, I'm not going to lie. I opted to take the medical route this time, and within days I found myself in a hospital bed, filling in paperwork, sobbing after two questions were asked by the nurse: 'Would you like a post-mortem, and would you like the remains back?' Can any mother ever be prepared to answer such questions?

In medical terms, those who die *in utero* within the first 24 weeks of life are termed as 'retained products of conception', so perhaps you should expect to be asked these questions while filling in a form. I am one of millions, however, who feel not. I know that for some people these aren't babies, they are merely a group of cells, and I respect that this is their opinion, but to me and my husband it was our child, not just a potential person, but a person, and he deserved to be acknowledged as such.

We were blessed to get pregnant for a sixth time and, after telling the family around the Christmas tree on Christmas Eve, I went upstairs to find I had started to bleed. The bleeding continued for days, and when I finally managed to speak to a GP I was told I had definitely miscarried, and there was no need for a scan. That crushing sadness overtook me again, and those who have experienced this first-hand will know you literally have to remind yourself to breathe; human functions just seem to disappear, as you feel you're free-falling over a ravine. I held on to the knowledge that to have my daughter would of course be enough, and that if we were never blessed with another child, we were one of the lucky couples who at least had the opportunity to raise one little girl. So we painted a smile on our faces and gave our daughter an amazing Christmas.

However, by 5 January, I was feeling so ill I decided to go for a scan, in case I needed another operation, and to our surprise they could still see a baby and all looked okay. I was told that this by no means meant all would be fine, but it was a good sign, and I should book another scan in a couple of weeks. During this time my sickness increased, and by the time I went for my next scan I was sicker than I had ever been while pregnant. The scan commenced and the doctor announced he could see two little lives on the screen. 'Yes, Zoë, you are having twins.' Cue me and Andy staring at him in shock and excitement in equal measure. He did warn us that one of the twins looked more developed than the other and that was not a good sign. With that information in mind, we were prepared (as prepared as one can ever be, that is) that we might not end this pregnancy journey with two healthy babies in our arms, but we prayed that we would.

Tragically, we did indeed go on to lose one of our precious babies, and we named her Isabella. Our other twin hung on, and we felt blessed to have one baby growing safely within, but heartbroken for the baby we lost.

What followed was a minefield of a pregnancy: I had to have my gallbladder removed, I had liver problems, placenta previa, my placenta was stuck to the old C-section scar, then the final blow came when I developed obstetric cholestasis, but our little warrior braved it all! When Bronte Jemima Hope finally appeared in all her glory in August 2011 she was declared a miracle baby, and I don't think we have stopped smiling since.

'Was it all worth it?' some may ask. Of course! 'Do you wish you had detonated your biological clock because it caused you so much pain?' Absolutely not. I have two wonderful little girls, whom I simply adore; they have made every single tear worth shedding. I'm so proud to be a mother, and I hope the trauma I have gone through makes me a better wife, mother and friend. My passion now is to raise my girls to love life and embrace every opportunity life hands to them.

What I have learnt through the heartbreak is this: to me, every child matters, however far in pregnancy a person is. I also learnt a lot about grief. I was a trained counsellor before going through loss, but quickly realised all the training in the world can't teach you what first-hand experience of baby loss does.

I learnt that everyone is entitled to grieve differently; some may not even feel a need to shed a tear, some may sob endlessly, and both are fine. For the heartbroken, however, acknowledging the loss is essential and it's imperative to both physical health and mental well-being to grieve. Life may never be normal again when you have been to such depths of darkness, but we can move forwards, with as little scar tissue on the soul as possible, and saying goodbye was the key for me.

I will never forget the thousands of couples who are so desperate to have a child and continue to search for the solution to their recurrent losses, and those for whom the miracle of conception just doesn't happen – all the people still waiting for their miracle to arrive. Whatever losses Andy and I have endured, we know we are truly, truly blessed to have two adorable girls to raise and hold.

To read my story in full, please refer
to my first book, *Saying Goodbye*.

PART 1

1

The Start of the Journey

What I would love this book to do for you is to help you see the value of grief in all of our lives, and for the words within its pages to teach you to accept its place rather than fight it – if we give grief a chair around our table, it stops it constantly knocking on our door without invitation. We need to see that grief doesn't have to be a monster living under the bed; it can be a gentle friend we don't need to run from. When we can see pain and grief like this, it lessens the grip it has on our lives.

One of the things I have learnt on my journey is how the way we view grief and loss, especially baby loss, depends on our personal views of death and life. If one values every life, whether it be short or long, that changes how we grieve and importantly how we live. If we want to embrace life, we also need to accept death; the two go hand in hand and if we can lose the fear surrounding this often taboo subject, we become more open to the emotions that grief and loss bring.

Let me start by looking at a key question: when should someone seek face-to-face professional support?

For some, professional help is needed immediately, others need it after a period of time has passed, and yet others never need it at all. Only you (and possibly your medical team) know when and if you require some additional support. There is an exception to this, and that is if you are suffering from post-traumatic stress disorder (PTSD). If you are suffering with this often-overlooked condition, you do need professional medical help. All the books in the world won't help you navigate this clinical condition, so if you have any PTSD symptoms please talk to your GP immediately. The quicker you get help, the better and more effective treatment can be, so delaying treatment is detrimental. Once PTSD is being treated, you will be able to effectively process your grief.

If at any point you feel hopeless or suicidal, please seek professional help without delay. People are not weak if they admit they need help, they are in fact the strongest of them all.

The Mariposa Trust asked 340 people about mental health and suicidal thoughts post-baby loss and these were the results:
* 49.41% of people had experienced suicidal thoughts.
* 47.06% of people were diagnosed with depression.
* 63.82% of people believe they suffered with undiagnosed depression.
* 69.12% of people said they suffered with long-term mental-health issues.

This is my general checklist to gauge whether people need professional face-to-face support, and a 'yes' answer to any of these questions would mean I encourage them to seek help (from a doctor, nurse, grief counsellor or clinical therapist):

1. Do you feel the waves of grief are getting worse over time?
2. Do you feel stuck in grief and are unable to move forwards?
3. Are you unable to socialise or mix with friends or family (feeling this initially is normal, but after some time a person should be happy to re-engage with the outside world)?
4. Are you suffering from panic attacks or anxiety that you are finding difficult or impossible to control?
5. Are you reliving the trauma on a regular basis?
6. Are you struggling to return to work?
7. Are you relying on alcohol or other substances to help you survive?
8. Do you feel vacant and removed from the world?
9. Are you struggling to eat or sleep?
10. Are you feeling desperate?
11. Are you avoiding things and feeling unable to face them?

If you have answered yes to any of these questions, please do consider getting some help.

THE EARLY DAYS

The early stages of loss are merciless, and to portray it as anything other than that would be unfair and untrue. The feelings are all-consuming and overpowering. They blindside you and can make you want to die, that is the bottom line. It is scary and unsettling and nothing can prepare you for it, but knowing it's 'normal' to feel these things helps, because when you are the one experiencing them you feel like you are going mad. So, let me reassure you, if you are feeling all these things right now, you aren't mad – you are heartbroken.

The Mariposa Trust asked 552 people how long the darkest part of their grief lasted following losing a baby, and here are the results:
* 0–2 months 11.66%
* 2–4 months 19.31%
* 4–6 months 17.49%
* 6–12 months 24.95%
* 1–3 years 15.85%
* 3+ years 10.75%

The initial days often go one of two ways. Either people switch to autopilot and just automatically do all the things that need to be done. They call people to inform them of the news, they make meals, they go through their checklist and carry out each task as if they are on a military assignment – this is the brain's way of surviving the initial trauma, and shock is helping them to carry on.

It's a basic human response that most are born with, a fight-or-flight response to trauma: if someone is about to attack us, we run, we get to a place of safety before we allow our brains to process what has just happened.

Or some people shut down. They aren't even able to do basic tasks, as their brain has just pulled the plug and said nope, I just can't go there – it is like a PC on an automatic shutdown. This can happen just for a few hours, but for some it's a few days. If it's longer than a few days, I would always advise the person to seek professional help.

Once the initial shock dissipates, the missing them kicks in. This void that they left in the world becomes a great big massive hole right in front of you, and you can do very little but stare at it. This is when the brain has realised the person is gone for ever and it has to come to terms with them being removed from your life. However much you felt prepared for the loss, nothing can actually help your brain deal with this period of time. I always say it is like a trap door has appeared and you suddenly fall. Life is okay one second, and totally changed the next. Every morning I would wake up and I would be hit with a fresh new wave of grief. There was no escape – every time a wave went over my head, it was like hearing the news that they had died all over again. A good description is probably this: it felt like I had been run over by a huge truck in a hit-and-run accident, but the lorry just kept coming back and hitting me again and again. Each time it would fling me into the air, and I would pray that was the last time it would make contact, but no, it would find me wherever I hid and hit me from a different angle.

The next stage is often a response to feeling out of control, and people may try to take control of things as much as possible. It can manifest as doing household chores, planning events (like the funeral), undertaking work projects, etc. It's the brain's way of trying to restore order. As it can't control the grief cycle and the feelings that surface without warning, it encourages you to take control of other things, which are probably completely unrelated to the loss, and at times can seem highly irrational to those surrounding the bereaved person. I will mention here that if you have any leanings to being OCD, this stage can be magnified.

WHAT TO EXPECT

Here are the emotional reactions that are widely recognised as symptoms of grief:

* Shock
* Worry
* Anger
* Guilt
* Regret
* Confusion
* Relief
* Disbelief
* Denial
* Sadness
* Upset
* Acceptance

I am sure you can list even more. Grief is a like a roller-coaster and a person can experience many different emotions and feelings in a 30-minute period, and this is what adds to that feeling of being out of control – you literally have no clue how you may feel from one minute to the next.

There are also many physical reactions, as grieving is a body, mind and spirit experience. Here are some common responses:

* Headaches
* Issues with sleeping – either too much or not enough
* Lack of appetite (or at times an increased appetite depending on your relationship with food)
* Nausea
* Stomach cramps
* Upset stomach (diarrhoea or constipation)
* Lack of interest in sex or physical affection (or at times an increased desire depending on your relationship with sexual intimacy)
* Anger or frustration outbursts
* Restless legs or numbness
* Racing heart or feelings of panic
* Nightmares
* Teeth or jaw issues (due to grinding of teeth or clenching your jaw)
* Hormonal disturbances
* Depression (which is different from grieving)
* Low immunity (which can mean you catch more colds and viruses)
* Iron or other vitamin and mineral deficiencies (often as a result of not eating well due to grieving, or blood loss)
* Dehydration – due to crying a lot and not replacing fluids
* Infertility

If you are concerned about any symptoms you are experiencing, please consult your doctor. While many physical symptoms can be linked to grief, it is very important to make sure there aren't other underlying medical conditions that are being overlooked, so please don't just assume that anything you are experiencing is connected to your loss; visit your GP to be on the safe side.

WHAT IS NORMAL?

Often people worry about what is normal, so let me reassure you that the following are common when grieving:

* Lacking motivation
* Feeling tired
* Inability to concentrate
* Inability to make decisions (sometimes even the most basic everyday decisions)
* Inability to remember even basic information and facts
* Feeling lost and like you aren't in your own body
* Lack of identity and struggling to remember who you are
* Unhappy or unsettled in your job (and questioning your career path)
* Uncertainty of key relationships and questioning how happy/satisfied you are with them
* Insecure about who you are or things you need to do
* Unstable emotionally
* Craving to be alone
* Craving to be with people and not alone
* Fearing the future
* Feeling impatient and having a much lower annoyance threshold
* Intolerant of things that never previously bothered you
* Feeling the world is unjust and unfair
* Fearful of carrying out normal tasks
* Fearful of death or losing other loved ones
* A desire to pack up and travel the world

COMMON QUESTIONS

When will these feelings end?

I get why people want to know this or how long the grieving process will take. I would have paid big money to find out the answer myself, but as grief is unique to every single person, there is no set answer. While this can be incredibly frustrating and also scary (as we all want to know the rollercoaster will end sometime soon), it can also be encouraging. 'How can it be in any way encouraging/helpful?' I hear you ask.

Well, we all know people who are stuck in grief and have never moved forwards, and when we are going through grief ourselves, we look at these people with eyes of terror, thinking that this is how we will now be for ever. But I can confidently say to you today, that's not how it will be if you don't want it to be – that is their walk through grief, not yours. You control your walk and you can heal; you can come out of the dark part of grief, and I hope this book shows you that.

What can truly help is to forget everything you have ever been taught or told about grief – for example, that the worst part of grief is the first week – because most of what we have been taught is sadly crap. The false expectation that we put on ourselves or others have put on us becomes the block over which we stumble, so remove it – throw it away. You will grieve for as long as you need to grieve and not a day less than that!

Should I ask my doctor for medication?

I am not a GP and won't even attempt to tackle this subject in my book. Some people need tablets to stabilise their emotions before grief can even start to be processed, while for others medication would prevent them from processing their grief. If you feel you need medication to help you (whether that be antidepressants or sleeping tablets), talk to your doctor. Your GP can and will help you. Please also be aware that if you have any past history with depression or any other mental-health conditions, grief can act as a trigger, so chat to your doctor as quickly as possible after suffering a bereavement.

When does the missing them end?

To be honest, I don't think the missing them ever ends, but in my experience it did get easier to live with. Once the shock had passed and life became normal again, those feelings just sat comfortably alongside everyday life, and I built my life around that hole, which can never be filled in. I think you adjust to it, as you don't want it filled in. Death made that hole appear, but love actually created it. It was only because you loved the person you have lost that the hole is that big and that deep, and that meaningful.

Grief is hard work, but if you can understand the process it is less scary. By learning about the patterns and associated symptoms, you can get to a point where you feel as if you are controlling it, rather than the other way round, as you are able to pre-empt potential waves and, when they do hit, you can be somewhat prepared.

I encourage you to be an active participant in processing your grief, and not just become a sitting duck. The more you consciously face the pain and the trauma of loss and grief, the quicker you will emerge from the blackest part of the grieving process. It is not going to be easy, or pretty – in fact, it is going to be the hardest battle of your life, and a billion tears may need to be shed – but you will survive it.

2

Loss and Treatment

There are many different types of baby loss, and I have included the most common types of loss in this chapter. If you have lost a baby via a different situation or condition, please don't feel I have forgotten you, and I hope all of the other chapters bring you the support and information you are looking for.

* Miscarriage
* Missed miscarriage
* Stillbirth
* Ectopic pregnancy
* Molar pregnancy
* SIDS/Cot death
* Neonatal loss
* TOPFA (termination of pregnancy due to fetal anomaly)
* Losing a baby through illness
* Losing a twin or multiple babies

As I am not a midwife, I thought it might be helpful to hear from one in the following pages, so I sought information from one of the UK's leading voices in midwifery, Kathryn Gutteridge, consultant midwife and president of the Royal College of Midwives. I ask the questions; she answers them.

I have also included stories from brave parents who have kindly shared their personal experiences with me, in the hope that those who are currently walking through this agony will feel less alone. I know that when I encountered loss I felt like I was the only person in the world who had experienced it, so that is why I wanted to share as many stories as possible in this book, so you know you are not alone.

Included here as well is a section on IVF and loss post-IVF. Fertility treatment and the feelings and emotions that surround it are complex, so I asked my friend and fertility expert Anya Sizer to contribute.

Miscarriage

What is a miscarriage?

A miscarriage in the UK is a loss of a pregnancy before the 24th week of pregnancy.

What is the physical and/or medical process of a miscarriage?

Miscarriage symptoms can vary from person to person. Often the first sign of a miscarriage can be pain in the lower abdomen, bleeding which may be dark blood but occasionally bright blood too. However, people can have these symptoms and the pregnancy is totally fine.

To confirm a pregnancy loss, a person may need to attend a hospital or clinic for tests. Tests may include: blood tests to measure the hormone levels, and an ultrasound scan which will usually be done by putting a probe into the vagina to see clearly if the pregnancy is less than 12 weeks, or on the tummy if over that.

If the pregnancy has ended and help has been sought, then the woman will be given medical advice about how to manage the next stage of the loss. Sometimes a woman may choose to wait for the miscarriage to fully happen without medical treatment, at other times a medical route may be taken.

Medical options include: taking medication to help deliver the baby and placenta remains, or an operation where the baby and surrounding tissue are removed surgically.

Depending upon when the pregnancy has ended, the management may be different.

What should a person be aware of during a miscarriage?

That miscarriage is not because the woman has done anything wrong. Many women blame themselves because they might have eaten or drunk something that they wouldn't usually when they are pregnant. Often an early miscarriage is due to some problem either with the development of the baby or with the placenta.

Although miscarriage is relatively common (one in four pregnancies end this way) society does not speak about it in a healthy way, so often families are reluctant to talk, but I would encourage everyone to share their experience.

What would be your best tip(s) for someone who has suffered a miscarriage?

Do not blame yourself — it is nothing that you did or didn't do.

How does someone know if they are bleeding too much post-miscarriage?

A woman should bleed as if she is having a light period (changing the pad four to six times in a 24-hour period would be considered normal). If there are any clots, that may be okay as long as the bleeding afterwards is light.

If someone has received poor medical care by a doctor or hospital, what should they do?

Firstly, contact the PALS (Patient Advice and Liaison Service) department in the hospital where they were treated and let them know the issue. There is one in every hospital and they should listen and be able to lead the patient through the complaints procedure.

What extra care can people expect or demand in subsequent pregnancies following repeated miscarriage?

All care should be personalised and responsive in future pregnancies. Maternity care in the UK is changing and a system of knowing a small group of midwives throughout the whole of the pregnancy, birth and beyond is beginning to take shape. This will help immensely with emotional support.

Why do hospitals not offer miscarriage tests until a person has had three consecutive miscarriages?

There is no good evidence that you must have had three miscarriages before you will be considered for testing.
In the UK, however, services are commissioned on a

basis that if it happens more frequently there must be an underlying problem. It is worth asking to see a gynaecologist who specialises in pregnancy loss and pre-term birth for more information.

✻ ✻

Emily's Story

I was delighted to find out I was pregnant that first time. It was a magical experience, seeing those two blue lines, knowing something wonderful was happening in my body and I was a mother.

Pregnancy hormones confirmed those fierce maternal feelings and I was very proud to have them. I don't know why – a habit in our culture – but I bought into that idea that I should keep this new identity of mine a secret until my 12-week scan, which was such a shame, because I never got to share how incredible and special that time was for me. I never made it to 12 weeks, I made it to 10, when I started bleeding, and 24 hours later it was confirmed that my baby had died and was coming away from me. It suddenly felt like my head was caving in. The sadness, the pain, the blood, the loss, the memories that would never be made, the baby names I'd considered that would never be written down on a birth certificate. And then, it happened again, again and again. I lost four children in the space of about 18 months.

Each positive pregnancy test after that first loss was much wanted but brought tremendous anxiety too – would I get to keep this baby? How long would I hold them; how much physical and emotional pain would I have to endure if I lost another child; why was my body getting it so wrong?

Losing multiple children was devastating and, with each loss, the hope that I would ever have a family got smaller and more bleak. My faith in life faded, my sense of safety in the world dissolved, everything went dark.

Bereavement (and that's exactly what it is) was deeply isolating, frightening, and made me feel angry, jealous, distressed and very confused. Friends tried to reach out and caringly offered, 'You know where I am if you want to talk.' But I was sure people didn't want to know what I was thinking – what I was thinking was not very nice. I was grief-stricken. So I just stopped talking to people. And I was allowed to disappear. One miscarriage seemed relatively manageable for people to respond to – flowers, cards, tea and phone calls. But after the second, third and fourth, people lost count. They didn't know what on earth to say to me and I didn't know how to make it easier for them to be around me.

Many of my friends at that time were busy growing their families and had healthy babies who were of similar ages to the babies I had lost. I couldn't look at those children without wondering what my children would have looked like, and I felt physical pain from not being able to hold them in my arms or see them with my own eyes. I became distraught at seeing other people's scan photos or pregnancy bumps. A woman next door to me was pregnant around the time of my third loss. I saw her pegging freshly washed sleep suits on the line in readiness for her new arrival. My heart became so very heavy I thought it would just drop out of my body.

It was traumatic emotionally, but also physically. People

don't talk about the biological reality of miscarriage. The blood; the contractions as you lose your child, even before 12 weeks; the ongoing morning sickness despite your baby no longer having a heartbeat; the various and frequent medical tests; the impact of dramatic hormone fluctuations; the ugly feeling in your gut and the trying to get pregnant again among all of this suffering and loss. I so desperately wanted a baby, a family, that I just kept on trying. Not really thinking (or caring) about the toll it was taking on me.

Difficult times really do highlight the resilience of your relationships. Wonderful women I knew who had also suffered baby loss were incredibly gentle and kind; they got it and I didn't have to explain or justify my distress to them. And then, my brother, of all people, he kept in touch with me regularly and just kept telling me he loved me. That is such a simple message. But there is nothing more that can be said. Love made me feel safer – once I had the space to let it in – and it was love that got me through that time.

I eventually had a successful pregnancy and gave birth to a son. My fifth pregnancy. It was an exceptionally nerve-racking time and, even after he was born, I was scared he would not stay. I don't think I really accepted that I would get to keep him until he was about six months old. But I am still the mother of five children: Pip, Dorothy, Anna, Ben and Leo. I got to keep Leo. It felt right to give names to my other children and mark their short lives with ceremonies and flowers. To pay them respect and love and acknowledge them as my children. They are part of who I am, they are part of my family, and they taught me to be a mother.

Ashley's Story

My wife and I have lost four children, two of them twins, and each one both before and after a healthy live birth. We have been incredibly blessed to get to meet four of our beautiful beloved children, who are all growing to be wonderful people of whom I am immensely proud, but we will never forget the four that never made it into our arms.

Parenthood changes a man, but miscarriage changes him in a different way. I have fathered four babies whom I never got to meet, and having become a parent without incident a year before our first miscarriage, it was never something I had considered should ever happen, nor was I aware of how common an occurrence it is.

My wife experienced the joy and elation of carrying our children in her womb for a few short weeks before the miscarriages occurred, becoming their mother and bonding with them; and then she experienced the unspeakable agony of that bond suddenly and inexplicably being ripped asunder. Miscarriage between live births is a unique experience in that, when subsequent healthy children are born, it doesn't feel like the miscarriage is cancelled out, but rather the grief stays with you, informing your parenting decisions. Fear of losing another child is heightened and this naturally forms the parameters within which subsequent children are raised. Miscarriage is not a one-time event, but something that indelibly and forever shapes the culture and character of the whole family.

A father's grief, at least in my case, is different from a mother's. Less intense, perhaps; less palpable. But the scars are real and the dull ache that resides in my heart, and goes unnoticed most of the time, is no less valid than any other grief, by virtue of the fact that a real person has been lost, as well as the potential for a unique, life-giving relationship to form having been snuffed out. The most profound impact of miscarriage is that any time a pregnancy occurs, you are just never sure how it will end up, and this, in my case, led to a greater degree of stress and anxiety throughout the pregnancies. I have attended three Saying Goodbye services, one for each of our occasions of miscarriage, and each one has given me the chance to outpour my grief and begin to heal.

Rebecca's Story

You see those two little lines on that pregnancy test and your life changes for ever.

Now before I go on, I should mention I'm married to a woman, something which in 2018 isn't unusual and normally I wouldn't feel the need to just announce it. But when it comes to having a baby, being married to a woman makes it harder. Once my wife and I decided we wanted children, we couldn't wait to get started. Now, I shan't go into details on how we managed it; all you need to know is there was a whole lot involved and the largest component was love.

But we managed it – in 2014, a few months after our wedding, I fell pregnant. It's amazing how much you can love something so instantly when it's barely even there. And then one day our excited happy journey turned into one of the worst moments of our lives. I had started bleeding.

We had an early scan arranged and were told things were fine. We could see a tiny but strong heartbeat; we were so relieved. We went home feeling a bit happier but still worried. Life carried on and then a few days later the bleeding started again. We had another scan but this time, sadly, we were told our baby had gone, I had had a miscarriage. I was inconsolable. We had just lost the most important thing in our lives, our very much wanted and already loved baby.

So that was that; we went home and had to deal with it ourselves. And by deal with it I mean you don't; you just carry on putting one foot in front of the other but feel numb inside. The pain is indescribable. We chose not to tell many people about our loss, just a select few. Mainly because I couldn't bear to keep saying the words out loud and, every time I did, I felt my heart break all over again.

After a short while we knew that we wanted to try again. So we did and thankfully I found out I was pregnant. We were so happy but somehow this time the horror of before dampened our joy. I was instantly terrified and reserved. Then once again came the blood. I couldn't believe it was happening again! So again we ended up back at the hospital. We knew what to expect this time and, as before, we were told that I had had another miscarriage.

Once again, we decided our want for a child outweighed our terror of going through it all again. But first we needed time to grieve for the two we had lost.

When we were ready once more, we tried – third time lucky. Eventually, after an agonising 12 weeks, we made it to our scan. And there on the screen, wriggling about, was our perfect little baby. We told the family our wonderful news and then we felt ready to tell them about the babies we had lost. Although to this day there are still some who don't know.

So nine (what felt like very long) months passed and we had our beautiful baby girl, Evie. She was and is perfect in every way. She has completed our family.

Missed Miscarriage

What is a missed miscarriage?

This type of miscarriage is diagnosed when the woman has had the usual signs of pregnancy and attends for her antenatal care or a scan, where no heartbeat is detected.

What is the physical and/or medical process of a missed miscarriage?

Pregnancy signs are well recognised by women, such as missing a period, and therefore many women can discover they are pregnant early by using pregnancy-testing kits, and so often presume all is well until their first scan. The commonest time to detect a baby has passed away is when the woman attends her first or second scan. It is then very clear that the baby is no longer alive.

What should a person be aware of during a missed miscarriage?

Of course, when attending their scan, women and their partners are not expecting to hear the news that their baby has died, and nothing can prepare them for this shock.

At times, some women may have had signs that the pregnancy was not well. This can be because the signs of early pregnancy have stopped, such as nausea and breast tenderness, and she may even have had some dark bloody discharge.

What would be your best tip(s) for someone who has suffered a missed miscarriage?

Do not blame yourself. You are not responsible for this loss, and while some people have a gut instinct something is wrong, more often than not people have no clue. Whether a person is or is not aware, it sadly does not change the outcome.

✦ ✦

Lauren's Story

In 2012 our lives changed when we were told, 'I am sorry, there's no heartbeat.' Five days later, I was induced and our son was born. I have blocked out many feelings, but I can also remember every moment of our journey, from hearing those words, to planning a funeral, having to explain to our other children, family and friends that our baby had died, and having to face the world again.

At 18 weeks our loss was classed as a late missed miscarriage. I will never forget someone saying, 'So, you just had a small bleed, then?' 'No,' I replied. 'I lost my baby. I gave birth and I have buried my son.'

I blamed myself and would often Google the causes of late miscarriage. But like many things, there is no reason, no one to blame.

I am lucky to have a very supportive family and friends, but at times I felt alone, like no one understood my pain, as though I was expected to be over our loss within months.

I now understand that my husband dealt with our loss in his own way; he returned to work not because he didn't care, but because his way of coping was to re-engage with life.

Just because he didn't want to talk about our loss or

didn't want to attend remembrance services didn't mean that he didn't care, or that he wasn't grieving too; he was just processing his feelings very differently from me.

For me, talking about our son is so important; sharing our grief and our family's journey is part of who I am now, and I couldn't even imagine not being open about our story. Losing our son was the hardest thing I have ever had to go through, but he has also made me a better person and changed me in so many positive ways.

Sarah's Story

My husband and I were travelling the world when we fell pregnant. A pregnancy test in Thailand, an early scan in Hong Kong, and then our baby came with us to Africa. At our 12-week scan in Zimbabwe, the sonographer broke the news of 'no heartbeat' as gently as possible. It felt like my heart had stopped beating too. We clung to each other and just sobbed. It's incredible how much you can love a tiny baby whose gender and personality you'll never know.

We were spun – in that dusty African street – into the admin of baby loss. The sonographer, knowing we weren't locals, drove ahead so we could follow her to the nearest GP surgery to discuss my options. I saw the world through a teary blur, as Jonny clutched my hand and the doctor suggested a pessary immediately and a procedure the following day. I wanted to hold on to that little body in my body a bit longer, but knew we needed to follow medical advice.

We were staying with my sister on her family's chicken farm, and returned to find a power cut – not an unusual scenario – and my sister waiting expectantly for beautiful scan photos. I saw her heart break for us as we broke our news.

That night, I began to bleed heavily. The doctor had told

me it would 'feel like a period, nothing to worry about'. That evening – just moments after the electricity had miraculously returned – I found myself screaming, 'He lied! He lied!' in the bathroom as the gruesome reality took hold. It felt nothing like a period. And everything like a death.

Amid my desolation was a flood of gratitude. We'd seen no family in nine months, and just happened to be staying with my sister when this all unfolded. We weren't on some remote Thai island. She brought us her low-battery laptop and highly prized imported Dairy Milk, and Jonny and I tucked ourselves away from the world under our mosquito net to watch *Big*.

At the local hospital the next day, I found myself acutely grateful for the NHS. Instead of a solid roof there was corrugated iron; instead of a clean gown I was given a threadbare old blanket; and instead of electricity, another power cut. I looked around at the local women in the waiting room and knew that if it was their lifelong medical reality, it would be mine for just one morning.

Our Little Adventurer is buried under a fig tree in the red African soil.

Stillbirth

What is a stillbirth?

In the UK, a stillbirth is when a baby at 24-week gestation or beyond has died in the womb or during birth. In the USA, it is when a baby over 20-week gestation has died in the womb or during birth.

What is the physical and/or medical process of a stillbirth?

Currently in the UK one in 200 pregnancies ends with a stillborn baby. This may be due to problems with the baby's development (such as genetic problems), the placenta not functioning as it should or the woman having a health problem which causes the pregnancy to end with a still-birth. Even with all of the causes that have been mentioned, occasionally there are stillborn babies where even after tests and a post-mortem no real answers can be found – this is very hard for everyone to understand. Stillbirths are mostly managed in maternity wards with both doctors and midwives. The shock of realising that a baby has died is without doubt one of the most devastating experiences that any woman and her partner can have.

If it is found that the baby has passed away prior to labour, the labour will often need to be commenced by medication so the baby can be delivered. The woman will be supported throughout the process until her baby is born. Following delivery, most maternity units allow the baby to remain with its parents so they can spend precious time together. It may also be possible for parents to take their baby home for a short time if they feel this will help with the painful goodbye.

What would be your best medical tip(s) for someone who has suffered a stillbirth?

Talk about your baby and your experience, as by talking you can process the grief.

＊＊＊＊＊＊＊＊＊＊＊＊＊＊＊＊＊＊＊＊＊＊＊＊

Jo's Story

I never had any issues with health and was fit and healthy. I got to 38 weeks pregnant and was getting ready for giving birth to our baby. We did not know what sex it was, to make it more exciting, so when on that Monday night in May 2010 my waters broke in the evening, with excitement we headed out to the hospital. I had so much water dripping down that my husband and I were laughing in the car and walking to the maternity ward, as I was leaving a trail of water behind me.

When we reached the maternity ward, they put me on a monitor and I could see on the nurse's face that something was wrong. She could not find a heartbeat and left the room to go and find the doctor. Our smiles turned into worry and when the doctor came in, which felt like a lifetime, he told us that we needed to move to another room to see the baby on the scanner. We went to the room, sick with worry, and our worst nightmare was then told to us. Our baby had died and there was no heartbeat.

It was nearly midnight at this time and I remember calling my mum and dad, who were waiting excitedly to hear the news, to tell them that there was just bad news. I still remember the scream that they let out, and they came straight to the hospital to be with us, together with my husband's family too.

We were told that we needed to wait till the morning before they could start to induce me as the staff was limited and, if anything went wrong with me giving birth, they did not want the risk. At about 5am the doctor came in, gave me an epidural and started the process of me giving birth. Once I was ready, it took 20 minutes as I just wanted to get the baby out and I pushed so hard that I burst vessels in my head. We told the nurse that we did not want to see the baby and so they put up a sheet. Once the baby was born, we were told it was a little boy, with thick black hair, and the cord was wrapped around his neck eight times due to being a very long cord. The doctors all tried to get us to see the baby and hold him, but we really did not want to and still to this day, eight years later, we are pleased that we did not see him. We just did not want the memory of what he looked like in our heads, as what we went through that night is a bad enough memory.

After a few hours, we came home with empty hands and I was in pain from pushing so much. The pain and grief were immense and I can still feel that pain today; it is something you never get over, but you just learn to deal with it. I was very lucky to have an amazing husband and family who were there to help give us the support we needed. Without them, I do not know what I would have done.

I have many moments and remember our little boy often. We never had a name for him, so have never named him.

After our little boy passed, three months later I became pregnant, which was the only thing that could get me through the ordeal. After a tough nine months I had a C-section at 37 weeks and went on to have a beautiful little girl, who was just our pride and joy. Another nine months later, I fell pregnant again and had another beautiful girl. This I am so thankful and grateful for, as they are our life.

Even though I have two beautiful girls, nothing takes away the pain of not having our little boy, but it did help with getting through the pain. I tell the girls about their brother and always wonder what he would have been like. Having the girls and seeing them, I sense that he would have been like them, with dark hair, just like my husband, as I am blonde and look like the nanny! I am sure that he looks over us and protects us and is the girls' guardian angel.

This year, I finally went to visit his grave for the first time as I could never bring myself to go and see him before, and I am pleased I did but very sad at the same time.

Gio's Story

We were so excited to be having a baby. We had our three-month scan, and all seemed fine.

Fast-forward to the early hours of 10 December. I remember being fidgety, and I nudged Chris to tell him I was going to have a bath. I lay in the warm water and it relaxed me a little, but little did I know that seconds later our lives would change for ever. I suddenly felt a lump between my legs, and I screamed for Chris. We phoned an ambulance, but they refused to come, and told us we needed to drive ourselves to the hospital.

We got into the car as quickly as we could and drove to the hospital. The doctor was quickly by my side and he scanned me. At this point I still thought we would be okay; I was running on adrenaline! The doctor then said the words that no one in the world prepares you for: 'I'm sorry, but there is no heartbeat – we need to deliver the baby now.' All I could say to the doctor, the midwives, and my husband was, 'I am sorry.'

Everyone tried to comfort me, but I didn't want comforting; I was in shock.

I decided I didn't want to see our baby girl at that point, I just wasn't ready.

My placenta then refused to be delivered so I was rushed to theatre. Lying on the bed in the operating room, seeing my name written on the board, felt surreal. Hours before, I had been relaxing in my bath, and now I had to face the horror of just delivering my dead child.

I was taken back to my room and we arranged for a priest to come in and do a blessing over our daughter. It was at this time I first cradled her in my arms. Tears streamed down my face, and it all felt totally surreal.

Later that night, Chris had fallen asleep and I sat looking at the memory box we had been given. Inside there was a book called *Guess How Much I Love You*, and I read this to my daughter. I wanted to read this book to my living child, not my dead child. I felt numb; I had plans and these were all now shattered.

The next day, it was time to say goodbye as we left the hospital.

Fast-forward a year and I sadly suffered an early pregnancy loss. This broke me further and pushed me to get the help I so desperately needed, and I finally got professional counselling.

Three years on, I can say time has helped me. I will never forget what has happened, but my lost children will live on in my heart for ever, and my quest for a living child continues.

Chris's Story

I learned I was going to be a dad in the August of 2015. I had just finished a particularly hard rugby match for my local team. My wife had come to watch and insisted we leave before I got into any post-match festivities. Walking back to the car to go home, my wife told me the amazing news – 'You're going to be a dad!' I was ecstatic and we couldn't wait to tell our parents.

The first scan at 12 weeks went well. The months went by and we were excited to welcome our precious daughter into the world.

Following signs of labour commencing, we went to the hospital. The umbilical cord had prolapsed so was starting to show, and, from here on in, our life started to fall apart.

The medical team were amazing and offered my wife such great care, and the doctor did a scan to check that the baby was okay. Tragically all was far from okay, as it was confirmed that our baby girl had died.

I consider myself to be fairly intelligent. I work in a hospital as an occupational therapist. I deal with difficult and stressful situations every day. However, my brain went to mush. I couldn't think straight. I could barely even talk.

However, the hardest call I had to make was to work.

It was the first time I had to say, 'We've lost the baby.' My work colleagues were amazing; they told me not worry about work and just to focus on what I needed to do. I can't thank my colleagues and line manager enough; they were very supportive and understanding.

I think men are never sure how to act in this kind of situation. You want to maintain your strength for your loved one during their tragedy; however, your world has also shattered and crumbled. My initial focus was on making sure my wife was okay, but there were times where I just sat and stared at the wall, trying to come to terms with what had happened. Tears. Anger. Terror of seeing my wife in such haunting pain. I experienced every emotion going.

Both of us returned to work and I found myself surrounded by pregnant women. I felt like life was laughing at me. Everywhere I looked, someone was pregnant or announcing that they were expecting, and here I was, a dad with no child to raise. Again my work colleagues were great, but I felt they were all treading on eggshells around me. It took me nearly three years before it started to get easier to deal with.

The bottom line was I'd lost my smile, nothing mattered to me. My friends tried to help but it was only a temporary fix until I returned home and thought about my daughter.

As time moved on, I found new ways of coping, but I have never returned to rugby as I have lost my competitive edge. But I found music to be a good catharsis and I now play in a band.

I would say I have now turned a corner – I am now more comfortable with this 'new normal'. I know it's a cliché, but I found it to be true – time really has been a great healer for me. My daughter will always be part of me and I will continue to talk of her for as long as I live.

Ectopic Pregnancy

What is an ectopic pregnancy?

An ectopic pregnancy is where the fertilised egg embeds outside of the uterus, typically in the fallopian tube. This happens early in the pregnancy.

What is the physical/medical process of an ectopic pregnancy?

The fertilised egg needs to embed in the deep, spongy tissue of the uterus. However, with an ectopic or tubal pregnancy this cannot happen. The baby will not develop because of the egg being in an unsuitable environment and this can cause harm to the woman the longer it goes unrecognised. About one in 80 pregnancies are ectopic.

What should a person be aware of during an ectopic pregnancy?

The first signs of ectopic pregnancy are missing a period and the woman assumes it is a normal, healthy pregnancy. However, very soon she will feel pain, usually on one side of her groin (corresponding to the implanted egg). She may also experience a watery brown discharge or even bright blood loss. This is a sign that something is not right. It is also common to experience pain when passing urine or when having bowel movements.

There could also be pain in the shoulder tip region; this is due to the nerves that are being irritated in the pelvic region radiating to the shoulder area. At times a woman may then collapse and this may be due to the tube being distended and blood loss.

What is the treatment for someone who is suffering with an ectopic pregnancy?

If a woman experiences any of the signs that may alert the doctor or midwife that this is an ectopic pregnancy, she needs to be seen quickly for assessment. This may mean an ultrasound scan to identify what is happening; the most common treatment for this type of pregnancy loss is surgery. Removing the baby is important (however heartbreaking it is) as the baby cannot survive outside of the uterus, and additionally the tube may rupture and cause the woman serious pain and harm. It may even be necessary to remove some or all of the damaged tube; however, it is possible for a woman to manage with one fallopian tube and still remain fertile.

What would be your best medical tip(s) for someone who has suffered an ectopic pregnancy?

Take time to recover and if concerned ask your doctor.

✷ ✷

Laura's Story

On Tuesday, 12 December I saw two red lines on a pregnancy test, for the first time. We had been trying for a baby for 15 months (including one round of the fertility drug Clomid in September) and had given up hope of getting pregnant naturally, so it felt like a Christmas miracle.

Within a couple of days, though, I began to worry something was wrong. I'd had a little bit of bleeding and discomfort on one side, which felt like a bad growing pain.

Two blood tests later and the nurse called to tell me my hCG levels (the pregnancy hormone human chorionic gonadotropin) were not doubling as expected and they were no longer treating this as an ongoing pregnancy. It was 21 December, with only one working day left until Christmas, so we had no choice but to wait it out and pray.

The happy news we had planned to share with our families on Christmas Day turned instead into tearful phone calls as we took it in turns to cry and rage. It's an experience I hope we never have to repeat.

We went back to the hospital just after Christmas – my hCG levels were rising but very slowly. A very invasive internal scan couldn't locate a pregnancy sack. My much longed-for pregnancy was now being described as 'of unknown location – can't rule out ectopic'.

When I shared the outcome on Instagram, one woman insensitively commented, 'I don't understand, so they just can't find it?' But despite what the scan said, I knew my baby had been there. I'd said goodnight to him or her as I rubbed my stomach; we'd made plans and bought Christmas presents from our little bean to each other. My hCG levels were rising right until the end; this baby was fighting as much as he or she could.

We were given the option to end the pregnancy that day or to come back in a week. Naïvely, perhaps, I thought this was a good sign, so we went to stay with my family for the week, all the time praying that our baby was just snuggled in somewhere safe and hidden. Now I know they sent us away in the hope the pregnancy would end naturally. Sadly, my hormone levels did not rise and we were left with no further option but to have the methotrexate injection, a drug which dissolves pregnancy cells.

I hated it. I cried as they administered the injection. But we could not save our baby; he or she was never going to survive and prolonging the pregnancy put my body and, potentially, my life at risk

The recovery was awful. By that point I had spent over two weeks going through the spectrum of emotions: tears, anger, despair, hope. Emotionally, I was drained. But physically I endured four more weeks of agonising stomach pain as my hormone levels slowly dropped, an ongoing, cruel reminder that, for now, I was still pregnant but would not be taking my baby home. One month on, my hCG levels were nearly at zero and we were finally discharged from the early pregnancy unit. One nurse assured me this was 'good news' but I couldn't see the good.

Because of the drug used for the injection, we couldn't try again for three months. I thought that this would be a nightmare; after all, we'd spent over a year focusing on having a baby, but it was surprisingly healing. It gave us time to grieve and spend time together, so when we started trying again in April 2018, I was in a much better place emotionally and mentally.

Andy's Story

When Laura told me she was pregnant I felt shock, disbelief, surprise but, overall, joy. Given we were due to go back to the hospital that day for further fertility treatments, it felt like surreal timing.

I am not an expert on pregnancy side effects, apart from knowing about the obvious morning sickness. So when Laura was bleeding and had some pain, I wholeheartedly believed that everything was fine and that it can happen in early pregnancy.

When I took the phone call from Laura, I was in a pub on my work's Christmas party. I felt for her having to break the news and tell me they expected us to lose our child. It was meant to be a day of merriment as we looked forward to Christmas and planned our lives as a family of three.

The two weeks of waiting for the results were nerve-racking and an emotional rollercoaster, but I just kept believing everything was fine.

The day of the injection was really hard. I am a fixer but I couldn't help Laura or our baby. To stand around physically fine while watching your wife in pain and grieving yourself is something no one should have to go through.

But the NHS staff were amazing and I was so proud of Laura's strength that day.

If I were to advise other dads in this situation, I would say: we can't do or say anything to help or solve the situation – all we can do is be strong for our partner. It is fine to grieve and you have to, especially with your partner, otherwise you can't build towards the future. Talking is key; break the strong male stereotype as it will get easier eventually with the support of those around you.

Molar Pregnancy

What is a molar pregnancy?

A molar pregnancy is not a pregnancy that the medical field is very familiar with as a lot more research needs to be done into this complex area of medicine. You can have a complete or partial molar pregnancy, and it means the fertilised egg implants in the womb but the tissue that starts to rapidly develop is not normal, and is known as gestational trophoblastic disease.

What is the physical and/or medical process of a molar pregnancy?

A molar pregnancy is actually classified as a tumour, which is a hard thing to hear and experience.

The tumour is actually a group of five separate tumours; one is benign (non-cancer) with the other four being cancer-forming. The non-cancer tumour is called a hydatidiform mole, which can be complete or partial and is formed of malformed chorionic villus tissue (the placenta-forming cells). The other four types of tumour are all formed of tissue from the trophoblast, which is the tissue that normally forms the placenta, but in this case it has malfunctioned to develop into types of tumours that are identified during surgery and tissue removal.

What should a person be aware of during a molar pregnancy?

It is difficult to identify a molar pregnancy and so it is often detected at the first scan. This type of tumour can grow quite quickly so it may be that it feels as if the pregnancy is further on than originally thought. However, some women experience severe sickness and nausea, and may have dark vaginal blood loss (sometimes there are what look like small grape-like lumps in the loss). If there is any concern or worries that a molar pregnancy may be taking place, the woman should seek advice as quickly as possible.

What is the treatment for someone who is suffering with a molar pregnancy?

The treatment begins with identifying what type of molar pregnancy has taken place and this will be done by carrying out an ultrasound scan and measuring the pregnancy hormones in a blood test. After this, a gynaecologist will explain the treatment that the woman is advised to undergo, which aims to take away as much of the tumour as possible. The treatment could be medication to expel the tissue, or, if possible, a suction method where a thin tube is placed into the womb and the tumour is removed by suction. Women are under a general anaesthetic for this method. If a woman has had all of her children, she may be offered a hysterectomy which removes the womb entirely so that it does not occur again.

After the surgery, the gynaecologist will recommend monitoring so that it does not return and this is usually by measuring hCG levels. This monitoring will last at least six months and may even be longer if levels of hCG remain raised.

What would be your best medical tip(s) for someone who thinks they may be suffering a molar pregnancy?

If experiencing any unusual feelings of the pregnancy growing rapidly, severe sickness and dark blood loss with smallish grape-like tissue, seek medical advice.

Jen's Story

In June 2014 my husband and I found out we were expecting our first child. It was nerve-racking and exciting.

The weeks went past and we told a few people. I thought, great, all I feel like doing is eating, not feeling sick, just hungry.

Our 12-week scan came along and we were excited to see the scan picture and revel in the fact that we were going to be parents.

We were called in and, as she was scanning me, I could see the screen and it didn't look like my friends' pictures that I'd seen. There was no baby, just an empty sac. The lovely sonographer said, 'I'm so sorry, you have had a missed miscarriage.' I sobbed, not knowing what to think or say. The rest was a blur. We had to have extra scans a week later and then they said I'd need an operation to remove what's inside.

It was a little odd as I had never had a general anaesthetic before. I was more nervous about that than what was going to happen. I was numb, and heartbroken.

After one month, in September 2014, I was called by the EPU [early pregnancy unit] to come in and discuss their findings. They said I had had a partial molar pregnancy and that I would need to do follow-up samples every two weeks of blood and urine to make sure my hCG levels went down.

Honestly, it was all a little too much for me to cope with, but I managed to give them what they needed, and thankfully by November all was good physically. Mentally I was a wreck but I tried to keep positive. The grief and sadness it has left me with has robbed me of all joy in early pregnancy, which I guess is a sad legacy of loss. Unfortunately, molar pregnancy is rarely discussed and most people have no idea what it is, so you end up having to educate everyone at the same time as grieving.

Lauren's Story

In September of 2017 we began to try for a baby. After three months, then five, then seven, I started worrying. Is something wrong with me?

It felt like it was taking for ever.

Then in April 2018 I started to get pregnancy signs. We were filled with butterflies and excitement and so ready! It felt like the most perfect timing! I was heartbroken during my ultrasound appointment when they couldn't find a heartbeat in a well-developed eight-week sac.

My doctor was confused as to why my unusually high pregnancy hormone levels and rapidly growing stomach didn't match up with my ultrasound. They said it would just be a waiting game because such high hormone levels often mean you are pregnant with multiples and they take a slower time to detect on ultrasound. They ordered me to come back every other day for blood testing and ultrasounds.

The next few weeks were such a crazy emotional rollercoaster.

We went in for an ultrasound appointment right before we needed to hop on a 12-hour flight for a job across the country and then another in Europe.

At this appointment, when I was lying down, I noticed the doctor's facial expressions start to drop. She said, 'It looks like your sac is collapsing. I'm so sorry. It looks like you are going to miscarry.' She decided to do one last blood test just in case and sent me on the flight with pills that would eventually induce the miscarriage if it didn't happen naturally.

I was absolutely devastated.

The airport security guard asked me if I was okay or in danger; I must have looked pretty distraught. I could never get myself to take a pill like that! The next day I got a text message from my doctor to call her ASAP! I called her and she said, 'Don't get on the flight to Europe or take that pill!' She told me to get another ultrasound immediately. She received my blood tests back and my hCG levels had skyrocketed! She said something is definitely growing in there and that it was most likely multiples because of how high my hormone levels were. She said there was a possibility it was a molar pregnancy but it didn't look like that to her.

I was praying with all my heart we were pregnant with twins!

It would be too expensive to fly back home, so we flew to Utah to be with my parents and go see a doctor there. When I went to get the ultrasound this time and she was feeling around my tummy, the nurse smiled. She said, 'So far it looks really good to me. There might be two in there!' I was so happy. She wanted to do an internal ultrasound to be able to see better. As she did, her face did the same familiar dropped facial expression as the nurse back home. She said, 'I don't know what's going on but it doesn't look good.' She showed us where the head and feet looked like they had started to form but weren't there any more.

I was so sad and honestly extremely confused about what this all meant. The doctor told me that this was extremely urgent and I needed to go to the emergency room right away. When I got to the emergency room the doctor there did another ultrasound, and said he wasn't a 100 per cent sure but it looked like a molar pregnancy. This means that instead of forming as a baby should, the cells had multiplied like crazy and were growing into a potentially dangerous tumour. He said he recommended me to have surgery right then to remove it. I asked him if there was any chance a baby could survive what he could see. He said from what it looked like to him the chances were 0 per cent. And he said if I didn't have surgery right away the chances for cancer and to not have kids in the future would increase. I said I just wanted to pray about it first with my mom and husband.

We prayed and came to the sad conclusion to terminate this pregnancy in hopes of healthier ones in the future. I was honestly relieved when my lab results came back as a molar pregnancy because I couldn't have borne to end a pregnancy this way knowing there might have been a chance. No baby can survive a molar pregnancy because the tumour becomes so widespread. Your risk for cancer, although highly treatable, is one in five. This meant I would need to be under close observation for the next six months to a year for cancer check-ups, and to prevent conception as well.

I think something that many are unaware of about miscarriage is the depression, anxiety, guilt and shame that comes along with it. I've been seeing a therapist and finding ways to cope with and heal this trauma and grief, and I'm proud of myself for admitting that I needed that.

If anything, this experience has taught me that life is a gift and pregnancy is a privilege. I want to move forwards knowing that, although you might never be the same, you can heal from pregnancy loss and have hope for the future.

SIDS (Cot Death)

What is SIDS (cot death)?

Sudden infant death syndrome – SIDS – is the unexpected death of a baby in the first year of life. In the UK about 240 babies a year succumb to this.

While there is not a great deal of evidence that SIDS can be prevented, there are some things parents can do to make it less likely. Sharing a room with a new baby is one of the best ways for parents to be aware of their baby's health; however, it is not advised to share a bed with a new baby. Making sure that a baby is placed on their back (not their front) can reduce the risk of a baby being unable to breathe (the Back to Sleep campaign). It is recommended not to smoke where a newborn baby is sharing the space, and women who do smoke are advised to give up in pregnancy to reduce the risks to their unborn and live baby. Some babies are more at risk than others, generally those born too soon, who are underweight for their age, where the mother is under the age of 20 years, and where the mother or both parents are using illegal substances and alcohol.

What should a person be aware of to try to prevent SIDS?

Sleep with a new baby in your room at night until they are around six months old. Never go to sleep with them in your bed (unless you are following safety guidelines).

✳ ✳

Caitlin's Story

At the age of 18, becoming a mum was never part of my master life plan, yet in May 2013 there I was, staring down at two pink lines, one faint and one strong. Three tests later and there was no change – I was pregnant!

Two weeks passed and I told my immediate family; after all, I needed their support now more than ever as I was no longer with my then partner. I had worked out that I was around 12 weeks, and so was booked in for an emergency scan. I attended with both my mum and dad, and as the screen sprang to life there was my baby wriggling in front of my eyes. The baby was in perfect health and all the relevant checks showed I was in fact 15 weeks and six days along. I had had no signs or symptoms, and suddenly was just about to hit the four-month mark of my first pregnancy.

Before we knew it, we were back in the scanning room, 20 weeks pregnant. Again, there was my baby, perfectly healthy, moving around on the screen. They asked me if I wanted to know the sex of the baby and I just couldn't resist – it was a boy!

My pregnancy was a whirlwind, and it felt as though it had ended before it had even begun. I finished work at

36 weeks' gestation, but at 37 weeks panic set into me as I could no longer feel my baby's movements.

I spent two long weeks back and forth to the hospital almost daily because I just couldn't feel his jabs and wriggles any more. They finally decided to induce me when I reached 39 weeks. It was a Wednesday – 30 hours after the process started, I was in labour. I was going to meet my little boy.

Seven hours and 25 minutes later, at 12.44am they handed me my little boy, Robert, who weighed a healthy 7lb 3oz. It was love at first sight, I can still remember him looking up at me for the first time; he had the most perfect deep-blue eyes and thick brown hair. We had plenty of visitors, and my mum never left my side. I was the proudest mummy taking him home.

Robert came everywhere with me. We went to Wales for my brother's graduation and down to Hastings for a few days' break by the seaside, staying in the caravan we used to have there. Before we knew it, Christmas had come around; he was spoilt rotten and had the most presents under the tree. My brother arrived for our 'second Christmas' on Boxing Day, and again showered Robert with presents and cuddles. We went to bed at around 10pm – not knowing of the nightmare that was ahead of us.

I woke up by myself on 27 December 2013, as opposed to waking up to the sound of Robert crying for his feed. As I looked over at my baby he looked grey, and was cold to touch. I screamed for my mum. 'He's not breathing, my baby isn't breathing!' All I remember is my dad taking him and calling the ambulance; my brother rushed to help and my mum stayed with me – it happened so fast but all I remember feeling was this numbness that I had never felt before. The ambulance arrived quickly and rushed me, my baby and my brother to the hospital. I was taken to another room shortly after arriving, while they did all they could for Robert. It felt like hours had passed, until a nurse came in and said the words I had been dreading hearing: 'I'm so sorry, we have done all we can but there's nothing more we can do.' I collapsed, my whole world had just crumbled around me, while less than 24 hours earlier everything couldn't have been more perfect.

I was thrust into a world of darkness, and a lonely feeling that I had never known you could have. I had booked and planned his baptism yet now I had to plan his funeral – the funeral of my eight-week-old son. Waiting for the autopsy reports was one of the longest waits of our lives; everything was closed for Christmas and New Year so it took even longer than usual. Once obtained, they provided no comfort to me as staring back at me was the information that I already knew: my baby boy was in perfect health and there was no medical reason for his passing, so it was put down to sudden infant death syndrome – nothing we could have done would have prevented this from happening. As a mum, all I wanted was to protect him as he grew, but I couldn't have ever protected him from this.

Neonatal Loss

What is a neonatal loss?

The death of a baby within the first month of life.

Why might this happen?

Giving birth prematurely is the reason most babies die in the first month of life; the cause is usually associated with their breathing, which has not fully developed. Approximately three babies per thousand will die in this way, according to UK statistics. The other main reasons for neonatal death are obstetric emergency, such as a cord coming before the baby; genetic conditions, disease or organ issues (e.g. heart problems). Finally, infections may overwhelm the baby and, because of its immature immune system, it cannot fight the infection even with treatment.

Why does premature birth happen?

There are some women who will be more at risk of premature birth. These may include women who have a medical problem such as diabetes or high blood pressure; women who are younger than 20 years or older than 40 years; women who smoke, use illegal substances and alcohol; or in cases of multiple pregnancy, infections or previous gynaecological problems.

One of the ways that services have tried to reduce the effect of premature births on babies is to have the mother in the right place for the birth. This may mean she is moved to another hospital where more appropriate neonatal services are located. This increases the baby's chances of survival.

❋ ❋

Catherine's Story

James Steven, 5lb 4oz and perfect, beautiful – an epic head of the very sweetest dark curls. My son. Our son. I still find myself wondering whether he was ever really here. The devastating thing about your child dying is that there are no stories to tell – or often the very briefest and most tragic story, so people stop asking you about your child who died because they want to avoid causing you pain (this, by the way, is the very opposite of how I'd like it to be – I relish every chance to talk about him and speak his name from my lips just as I do with my other two sons). So it can seem at times that they are a fable, somehow mythical and ethereal because there is just this lost story of birthdays they never had, Christmases they never shared, first words, steps – all there is that never happened.

He came in a sudden chaotic panic of medical processes – born with a bilateral pleural effusion, which I was assured was perfectly treatable and relatively minor in the list of possible complications a baby could face. Just as quickly as he arrived, he was gone – just 77 minutes after birth.

It was a dreary, nondescript kind of day, except it was a Friday – Friday the 13th. I could hear the doctors talking and could hear them desperately trying in vain to save my son.

I looked at my dad who was with me in the delivery room (my husband was at home looking after our two-year-old, as I had only gone to the hospital to have a routine scan) and I said, 'It's not going to go our way, Dad.' Something inside me just knew that he couldn't be saved.

What followed was terrible, inhuman screams of despair (apparently it was my voice although I didn't recognise it), sobs, tears, shaking, a body racked with physical pain from the emotional burden that it just could not bear. There were sad words, wrung hands and people, strangers, everywhere. I felt utterly robbed of my son and tortured that his future would simply not exist.

After he was born and after his death the aftershocks just kept on coming. The constant questions were unrelenting. Everything from questions about post-mortems to funeral arrangements. I wanted it to stop. I wanted no part of this. This was not the life I was supposed to have and this shouldn't be happening to us because this was not my life, our life.

I spent hours watching TV with no sound on, avoiding everything from moving to eating to seeing anyone or talking on the phone. I refused to participate because it was as if I was watching from the outside in, no longer a participant but an unwilling spectator.

But. And it's a big one – early on, very early on, I looked at this vast and imposing Lincolnshire sky above me and I made a promise that I would live life in his honour and make him proud of me. I knew I wanted, no, had to smile again because smiling is just what I do. Smiling is who I am. Talking to my dad I said, 'Dad, I've got to be happy again for Steve (my husband) and Joe (my eldest child, two at the time)', and he said something I'll never forget. Not ever. He said simply, 'No, Catherine, you have to be happy for you.' He was right.

Slowly, and I am unsure how, this need and hope I had that one day I would once again give a real, genuine eye-wrinkling smile gave way to actually doing it. Smiley me was back. Once my husband had returned to work, I just had to show up for life again. Explaining to a two-year-old that the park was closed, or ignoring the need for nappies, or the demands for food and playtime, clean clothes or whatever whimsical wish he made – the mundanity of life just kicked in and I had to be a functioning mummy again. My needs were indisputably trumped by the need to be a mum to Joe. And so slowly, very slowly, I saw people again. I left the house and went to the supermarket because those home-cooked meals that kept landing on my doorstep (thank you, friends) just weren't going to keep coming for ever. Life took on its interminable whirr of just 'doing'. Life was different. It still is. Everything has changed.

After a difficult third pregnancy another son arrived in our arms. Baby Edward showed us once again that life needed to continue forwards and he brought us a beacon of hope.

Every happy moment I've ever had since James was born, I've found that he's naturally been in it – at least in my thoughts and my heart because that is my way of bringing him in and keeping my eternal love for him woven through-out my life. James is my point of reference because there was a before James and an after James. There was a life before him and a life after and I am deeply changed by him – we all are. But it is my great hope that I am a better me and I no longer underestimate my own strength or abilities.

TOPFA (Termination of Pregnancy due to Fetal Anomaly)

What is a TOPFA?

TOPFA is where an anomaly (life-threatening or life-altering condition) is identified and a parent makes the incredibly difficult choice to end the pregnancy.

Terminating a pregnancy where an anomaly has been identified is an area of maternity care that is usually managed in the fetal medicine department. A specialist team of obstetricians who are able to interpret complex ultrasound scans and specially trained midwives look after women and families at this time.

What is the physical and/or medical process of a TOPFA?

A very detailed discussion should take place with the family before a plan can be made for a termination of pregnancy. This is not an easy decision for any family to make and the team will allow the family to take as much time as they need and it may be performed at any time in the pregnancy. If the pregnancy is more than 22 weeks, a process is offered to stop the baby's heart beating – another medical name for this procedure is 'feticide', which ultimately ends the life of the baby in the womb. This will be performed by the fetal medicine obstetrician and a specialist midwife using an ultrasound scan and a solution that the doctor injects directly into the baby's heart. Following this, the woman is given medicine so that labour will start in a similar way to other methods of inducing labour.

However, some women prefer to give birth to their baby and to have their baby die in their arms. If this is the case, a detailed plan of care is prepared to ensure that no mistakes are made in the baby's initial response to life. This plan should be discussed fully with the woman and her family so that they are in agreement.

What should a person be aware of during TOPFA?

Words are important and therefore only skilled clinicians should be involved in this procedure so that the family have the most experienced people around them. The drugs that are used to induce labour do not work immediately and some women prefer to go home and wait for labour to start. These drugs stop the pregnancy hormone progesterone being produced and after a period of time the cervix (opening of the womb) starts labour. Unfortunately, for some women labour can take a few days to start and be over.

What would be your best medical tip for someone who has had a TOPFA?

Take all the time you need before making a decision about what your next steps should be and don't let anyone rush you. Feel free to ask for a second or even third opinion if you want to; there is no shame in asking for more medical views.

Seek independent counsel and look at several sources of information. Some websites are written to steer you in certain directions; be savvy to this by looking at as many sites as possible.

Extended families often want to advise and make things better for a couple going through this; it is vital that the couple are able to reach their own decisions.

✴ ✴

Sarah's Story

We found out at the 20-week scan that something was wrong. Our daughter had a rare fatal heart defect called cardiomyopathy and we were told her condition was so severe that nothing could be done to help her. Within 24 hours we went from expecting a healthy baby to being told we wouldn't bring her home alive.

After monitoring, we decided to opt for a TOPFA (compassionate termination) to ensure she would not suffer any pain at delivery or birth, one of the hardest decisions I have ever made. How do you lie back as a mother and let someone kill your much-loved baby? Even now I still don't know the answer and carry a huge amount of guilt and pain. I felt her moving in the weeks before she died – each time was filled with both joy and agony. It was the hardest month of my life.

It's neither simple nor quick to terminate at 23 weeks and four days' gestation, and after she died I went through seven hours of labour before I could hold her. I know she would have died regardless of the choice we made, but it doesn't make it any easier to live with. I was her mother and yet I couldn't protect her. It was explained once that our choice ensured that any physical pain she might have suffered was transferred into emotional pain that we would likely carry for ever. A burden we chose, to spare her any pain. Explained in this way, I can take a little comfort in knowing that we did the right thing for us as a family – I would happily carry this pain forever for her. I just wish my heart would stop breaking.

I tell her often that I miss her, that I love her and that I am sorry. I hope that she forgives me and maybe one day I can even forgive myself.

Nick's Story

We couldn't bear to look at the ultrasound screen. My wife's hand gripped mine. She was lying on a bed in a small room while the consultant prepared an injection that would gently stop our baby's heartbeat. It was not something we could watch.

Almost four weeks earlier, we couldn't look at anything but the screen. It was during the 20-week scan when we were told that something was very wrong. It took an unbearably long time for the nurse to speak. Over the next few days, it became clear that the daughter we already loved was desperately unwell. Her heart was not beating as it should. As a dad, there was nothing I could do to help our baby or protect my wife, which was a horrible feeling. But we clung on to the hope that there might be an improvement. We had more appointments with a specialist paediatric consultant. But her heart didn't get better, it got worse. We had to face the awful truth that she was fading away. Still we waited a little longer, hoping for a turnaround. But it never came. Her condition was deteriorating and we were told she would die, if not before birth then soon afterwards, with all the struggle and pain that would entail.

It was agonising for my wife to be carrying a baby inside

her that we knew was dying. It wasn't just mental and emotional torture but there was an increasing medical danger to Sarah too.

Once we'd made the decision to let our daughter rest, everything became harder, not easier. It was like being crushed under a wave and fighting for breath underwater.

So there we were in a small room, awaiting an injection. We know we did the right thing, to save her from struggle, but it's a decision I wouldn't wish on any parent. And I just wanted to close my eyes.

Losing a Child Due to Illness or Accident

There are thousands of reasons why and how people lose their much-loved child post-birth, and it would be impossible to cover them all within these pages. The Mariposa Trust supports people who have lost a baby in pregnancy, at birth, in early years, right up to four years of age. One common thing I hear people say – however old their child may be when they sadly die – is, 'I lost my baby' (I hear this even from those who have lost adult children), and this is one of the reasons why the charity expanded the support it offers to families who lose a toddler and small children.

Here I wanted to share two families' stories of loss. The first is Nicole's – she sadly lost her son through a tragic accident. Then we will hear from Jennie and Matthew, who share their experience of losing their daughter Elea following her battle with leukaemia.

✤ ✤

Nicole's Story

Our second son Ben was born happy and healthy at 39 weeks. He had the loudest scream – thank you, reflux – but the warmest smile, and he had me wrapped around his little finger. He was 100 per cent a daddy's boy and adored his big brother; every day he was told how much we all loved him. But on a cold Tuesday morning in November our lives were changed for ever.

Having just moved to Scotland, I was on a mission to make mummy friends, so I took Ben and his older brother, Alistair, to the local toddler group. The morning was a huge success; the boys played, and I met other mums. At the end of the session I secured Alistair into the toddler seat on the top of the pram and slid Ben in his bassinet underneath. Ben was exhausted and fell straight to sleep. As his eyes closed, I remember the look he gave me: pure love. I had no idea that would be the last time I would see his eyes; it is a moment I will treasure for the rest of my days.

After loading the pram up with shopping and visiting the local charity shops, I secured the rain cover over Ben's part of the pram and we walked home. When I got to my friend's front door, I went to get Ben out of the pram, but that is the second our lives changed for ever. In the brief

10-minute walk home, the chicken for tea had slipped off the hood of the pram and landed on his face. Ben was not breathing; he was blue and floppy.

The smallest decision destroyed our world.

After giving Ben CPR, and my friend going and getting help, we were able to make him pink again but unfortunately the damage was done. Later that afternoon my husband and I were informed that Ben was not responding to treatment. We had to make the decision that no parent ever wants to have to make. We had to turn off our own son's life support. At 4.30pm on 13 November 2012 Ben took his last breaths surrounded by the pure love of his mummy and daddy. It was the most peaceful moment I have ever experienced and one that changed our world for ever.

When Ben died we lost a future with him in it. We lost all the hopes and dreams we had, not only for him, but for our own lives as well. We lost who we were as parents, as a couple, as individuals. We lost our innocence. The safety of life is taken away once your child dies.

Child loss, in any form, is a taboo. It is against the natural order of life, so we try to make sure that we are safe, and we try to make sure it never happens to us. All any parents want is to be able to take their baby home, because getting them home means they are safe. But what happens when you are the parent whose child has come home safely, was healthy and had a long future ahead of them, but dies in a freak accident?

You become the ultimate taboo! Why? Because if people acknowledge your existence, they will never feel safe again. Child death is the elephant in the room of any culture, but accidental child death is the elephant in the room wearing a tutu and shooting sparkles out of his trunk.

So how do you live, being the sparkle-shooting, tutu-wearing elephant?

We started at the very foundation of our lives, our marriage. My husband and I made a pact – that we would not give up on each other. The hardest thing that we have had to do is trust that we never mean to hurt each other. Living with grief is like living with an open wound; some days the scab is hard and it doesn't hurt, but other days your wound is open and raw. You must be gentle with yourself but also trust that others don't mean to make the wound worse. We take each day at a time and we tell each other, and those around us, when we are struggling.

Our families have learnt that we love talking about Ben; saying his name helps our grief. Talking about Ben helps heal our hearts. We will never be the same again, I have changed to my very core, but I am still a mum, I still love my child and I will always want to talk about him just as I want to talk about our other children. When I tell people about my son, I see fear in their eyes and that makes me sad. It breaks my heart a little bit more every time that people can't see past his accident. Ben was a beautiful boy who is loved and deeply missed. I don't want him to be remembered for how he died; I want him to be remembered for how he lived, all 122 days.

Jennie's Story

It was the day after Mother's Day, 27 March, after a week of my 15-month beautiful, clever little girl, Elea, just not being herself. I took her to the GP after seeing a rash on her arms.

The doctor I saw was so lovely but obviously concerned. She told us we needed to go to hospital immediately. We arrived and waited. A cannula was put in her little hand and blood was taken.

She was so pale and sleepy. My husband joined me by lunchtime and by the evening we were admitted for the night. About 10 minutes later, six doctors and nurses came into our room. My heart sank. 'We are so sorry but your daughter has leukaemia. We are not sure of the type yet but she needs extra fluid and a blood transfusion.' I cried with the heartache, the heartbreak. We were in shock. How could this be happening to my 15-month-old little girl, my longed-for baby?

After three weeks in hospital, three general anaesthetics and lots of different medicines, we finally had a diagnosis of acute myeloid leukaemia and we were off to the Royal Marsden children's ward in Sutton, where we started her first round of chemo. Nothing quite prepares you for consenting to your child being given the worst drug in the world. It makes you grow up rather quickly in that moment.

Acute myeloid leukaemia is one of the worst types of leukaemia you can get; it is particularly horrible in that it affects young children. The treatment is usually six rounds of chemotherapy, but if the first round goes well you could be into remission quickly.

Elea, our precious daughter, had possibly the worst sub-type of AML, with similar characteristics of another blood disease at the same time. Her first round of chemo looked really positive and for the first time in eight weeks we were allowed to go home! It was a glorious week. Seeing friends, having her hair cut, getting her first shoes. And just being slightly normal despite being the nurse and her mummy.

We came back into hospital and to our delight we got our own room. But the news we heard was not great. The leukaemia had not gone into remission and we were now on the stem-cell transplant route.

The journey in hospital was one of hope, joy and anguish. Elea had five rounds of chemo, six general anaesthetics, 25 feeding tubes inserted, numerous antibiotics and other medicines. She was an absolute trouper, who owned the corridors of the children's ward with her walker, whose smile and wave would grab everyone's attention. The nurses were outstanding and fought about who was going to look after her. Our friends were championing us with food, visits, presents, prayers, chats. But after six months in hospital and only nine nights at home, the leukaemia was too strong.

At 12.30pm on Sunday, 10 September 2017 our darling daughter went to heaven while in my arms. My husband and I were broken and shocked; we would never be able to hug her again, hold her hand, play with her, see her grow up.

Grief is a rollercoaster of emotions. You never know what you'll be like from minute to minute, hour to hour. Life is truly unfair. I can remember a moment in hospital towards the end when I just knew we weren't going to have her for much longer. I couldn't stop the tears, they just kept coming.

A year has passed and I certainly can't believe it has. I feel there are days when I miss her more than ever and just want to be playing with her, doing mummy life. Life will never be the same.

I want to finish with an anonymous quote that sums up how I feel most days:

'Grief, I've learnt (am learning), is really just love. It's all the love you want to give but cannot. All of that unspent love gathers up in the corners of your eyes, in the lump in your throat, and in the hollow bit of your chest. Grief is just love with nowhere to go.'

Matthew's Story

(A FATHER'S EXPERIENCE)

Elea had an occasional temperature or sniffle and one short brush with chicken pox. That was it. While friends and family with children had an almost constant stream of coughs, colds, bumps, bruises and all the rest, when social media was announcing yet another bedridden family, my wife Jennie and I couldn't help but feel very lucky that our (eventual) bedtimes were purely due to sleep rather than anything else.

Elea had been a very happy and very healthy little girl for nearly all of 15 months when we were told, in a room with a multitude of doctors and specialists standing around us, that she had a rare subclass of acute myeloid leukaemia (AML). There were treatments, but it wasn't going to be easy and the outcome was far from certain.

So many emotions ran through my head; fear overriding every one. My own hope was that we could do this, Elea could do this. Would I be the husband and father my girls needed, now more than ever? Would I be strong enough? What would we do if she didn't make it? I like to think that I am a positive and optimistic person, but faced with this news, a sucker punch to my heart and soul, I just didn't know if I could do it the way I wanted to do it and Elea and Jennie needed me to do it.

It's hard to be positive when facing fear head-on. My wife and I are normal people; we're not necessarily any stronger than any other man or woman; we did what we had to do in those six months – we called it 'survival mode'. We did what we could to make our little girl happy; we cherished every moment we could. I don't think we had a choice to do anything else. Our bodies and minds wouldn't let us.

Elea endured five rounds of chemo, each one more extreme than the last. Unfortunately, the treatment just wasn't enough and we entered into palliative care, staying at the hospital so we could just look after Elea without the burden of having to nurse her, as well as be her parents. This lasted just one week. We let our little girl go to heaven on a Sunday morning, cradled in her mother's arms, with me holding them both.

Our consultant had reassured us that it wasn't anything we or she had done, it was just something that happened; but it is extremely hard to rationalise an illness that came out of nowhere, with no warning. It just didn't seem fair, any of it.

The weeks following our loss did not consist of much beyond trying to hold things together and remember to eat and drink, and planning a funeral we had never expected to plan. A massive network of friends and family helped us through this time (and continue to) and have made our devastating loss that little bit easier to bear.

I don't think anything you do in grief is necessarily right or wrong, you just react, you do. You get through each second, minute, hour as best you can and, whatever decision is made, that's it. We both have treated our loved ones unfairly, been angry for the smallest of things, got upset at a song on the radio, but at the core of all these missteps is our loss. It's not an excuse but more an explanation, and I believe it is getting easier, whatever that means. We have had counselling, we have family and friends helping us, but one thing we do know: it's not a journey with a fixed timeline; I don't believe it will ever be 'completed'. It is a process and burden that will always be with me, with our family. Elea will always be missed and life's milestones will be forever bittersweet, but all anyone can do is keep moving on and try not to forget the precious, golden moments of her short, beautiful life.

Losing a Twin or Multiple

Losing a twin or a multiple is heartbreaking and can involve a host of other feelings during the grieving process. Society seems to expect you to just carry on if you have a living baby/child to focus on. As a parent you are wanting to celebrate the living baby, while simultaneously grieving for the baby(ies) you have lost, and it can be incredibly hard to juggle both joy and grief at the same time.

I have personally walked through this as we lost our baby Isabella, who was Bronte's twin, during pregnancy. You can learn more about that in my first book, *Saying Goodbye*, so here I will let Jess share her story.

✳ ✳

Jess's Story

I was 29 weeks pregnant with twin girls when the sonographer told me that Harriet's heart had stopped beating. My pregnancy was being closely monitored because of absent end-diastolic flow (AEDF) through Harriet's umbilical cord. I knew that my babies were growing at different rates but I had been comforted just two days before by my midwife, who had assured me that she could detect two clear heartbeats. I hoped and prayed every day that both my babies would be delivered safe and well. Each time I felt the flutter and prodding of their little kicks I felt closer to them, and held on to the faith that all would be okay. 'Do excuse me but I just need to pop out of the room' were the words of the trainee sonographer that day. It was then that I knew. One of my babies was dead. I recall the song on the radio as we drove away from the hospital – 'Together in Electric Dreams'. The same scan had shown Josephine's heart beating strongly and I was comforted knowing she was growing well, but I was terrified she would die too. My world had changed. It was as if someone had switched off the light.

The final few weeks of my pregnancy remain lost to me, in a haze of fear, worry and confusion. I was pregnant with twins, yet only one was alive. I carried both babies but felt only one pattern of kicks. Only one set of hiccups. Josephine's movements had become so familiar to me yet I felt so robbed. It felt so unfair. So unjust. The family I thought we were to become had changed overnight and all my dreams associated with it turned to dust. Obliterated before they had begun. One of the hardest things was telling people that one of my babies had died. I felt I should be thankful for Josephine and that I should 'just get on with things'. I almost felt that I had no right to feel so bereft. Friends knew I was expecting twins but I didn't know what to say or how to say it. So, rather than telling people, I often retreated and didn't say anything at all. Seeing other pregnant women was difficult for me and I found knowing others were pregnant with twins very upsetting. I had an internal battle going on inside my head — was it okay to feel so blessed with my baby yet also mourn the death of my baby at the same time? I felt guilty feeling happy and guilty feeling sad. Such a conflict of bittersweet emotions. My heart felt heavy.

My girls were delivered via Caesarean section when I was 37 weeks pregnant. Harriet Grace was delivered first, silently. I remember the deafening silence in the operating theatre, if only for a few seconds. Then I heard the hushed close of a door. I lay motionless and devastated, knowing the midwife had swiftly taken my dead baby to the morgue. My body felt numb. Anaesthetised by the spinal block and desensitised by the fear of delivering a dead baby. My dead baby. Then, the silence was pierced by the life-affirming scream of Josephine Grace. Covered in vernix, trembling with life and eyes screwed up so tightly, my baby was raised up from behind the screen and placed in my arms. Weighing 6lb 4oz. Safe and well.

I nursed Josephine but my body ached for Harriet. I smiled because my baby was with me but I wailed because my baby was dead. I smiled because my baby was perfect but I wept because my baby was in the morgue. I smiled because I had finally met my baby but I sobbed because I would never meet my baby. My heart burst with joy when my three-year-old daughter met her new baby sister but it shattered into a million tiny pieces at the same time. Shards of glass.

My grief was buried deep and didn't start to surface for a long while. In the early days, I hid the pain from the outside world but it carved its place in my heart. Anger surfaced whenever I saw twin prams and feelings of jealousy ambushed me. I felt robbed of the chance to be a mum to twins and I avoided getting into conversation with new mums. It was too painful. It felt as if I was keeping Harriet a dark secret but I knew she had the right to be honoured and remembered. My baby was real. She had lived yet she had not taken a breath outside of my body and few people knew of her delicate existence. Did I have three children? I wasn't sure.

Seven years on, I imagine what it would feel like to brush her hair, breathe her in and hear her call me 'Mummy'. Writing Harriet's name on the page and saying it out loud is a comfort to me. It's proof to the world that she existed, if only for a short time. We scattered her ashes in a peaceful place and I visit every now and then, feeling the gentle breeze on my face. There are times such as birthdays, celebrations and milestones when I feel a surge of emotion and it often takes me by surprise, knocks me sideways, but the love I feel for all three of my daughters stops me from falling.

I chose not to see Harriet. Instead, I asked the midwife who delivered her to describe to me how she looked. I questioned my decision over and over again for many months afterwards. It played on my mind, but the torment gradually began to subside and I know I made the right decision not to see her. Her handprints, footprints and a few little wisps of her dark soft hair are cushioned carefully in a little box. My daughters and I occasionally talk about Harriet and I am trying to help them to understand. In time they will.

Over time, I have learnt that grief is unpredictable but it has to be worked through, however that might be. If you shut it away it is still there and will creep out eventually. My world has been rocked in a way I never imagined, but I have somehow found the strength inside. I am a stronger version of myself now. When I reflect, I close my eyes, inhale deeply and remember how far I've come. I remind myself of how much life there is yet to live and how blessed I am to be raising my children. I smile and my heart feels lighter.

I didn't lose a baby. My baby died before she was born. She was and always will be part of me. She's right here. Her little life was a gift so rare and irreplaceable that I hold it close to my heart every single day. Together in electric dreams.

IVF and Loss Post-IVF

IVF and fertility treatment is a very complex subject and I could write a separate book just on the issues and experiences people face. If a person loses their baby post-fertility treatment it adds an extra layer of trauma to the experience, and this is something rarely discussed. I asked fertility expert Anya Sizer some questions about IVF and loss post-IVF.

What is the process of IVF?

In vitro *fertilisation has been around for 40 years now and is an incredible science. It provides a way for those with sub-fertility issues to conceive by creating an environment where sperm and eggs can fertilise outside of the woman, creating embryos and hopefully allowing conception to occur. There are many different types of IVF, or protocols, but the essence of it is always this:*

A cycle will first try to create a good number of eggs from the woman via injections to stimulate the ovaries, the exception to this being natural-cycle IVF which will follow a woman's normal cycle and usually only be looking for one, possibly two, eggs each cycle.

The egg or eggs must then be removed via a trigger shot, followed by egg retrieval under heavy sedation. Once the eggs have been removed, the sperm is either introduced into the Petri dish and allowed to fertilise the egg or is injected directly into the egg to encourage fertilisation (ICSI). We would then hope to see fertilisation and growth occur within the embryos and around three to five days later an embryo transfer can take place.

There then follows the hardest part of any cycle – the two weeks' wait when a patient must act as though pregnant while not knowing if the treatment has indeed worked. Psychologically, this is exhausting and can be a time of real anxiety. At the end of the wait, a person will do a blood test or home pregnancy test to see if the treatment has been successful.

Why do people need to have IVF?

Although infertility is still seen as a woman's problem, much of the time it is in fact evenly split between male factors and female factors or unknown reasons.

Male problems tend to focus on sperm issues or blockages. Women's reasons can vary from issues around egg quality, womb lining or hormone problems. Sometimes IVF can be needed for an obvious reason such as a blocked fallopian tube in the woman. However, there are increasingly 'unknown' causes for needing treatment, which can be incredibly frustrating to the person.

Certainly, an increase in the age of women first trying to conceive is a factor. In my experience, the main reason women are having children at an older age isn't due to their career (which is often how it is portrayed in the press); it is more often due to not finding a partner until later in life.

The reasons for needing treatment are hugely varied and cut across all social groups and demographics.

Are there other options available apart from IVF?

Yes, many people will start off with ovulation-inducing drugs such as Clomid and then try IUI (intrauterine insemination) before proceeding to IVF. Often people will attempt to go down a more holistic route first.

How long is the IVF process?

An IVF cycle varies in length depending on the protocol and how long someone will take to respond, but would usually be around six weeks.

Are you pregnant from the moment transfer happens?

This is a really difficult question and will depend on who you ask! Certainly, in terms of the law you have the right to be treated as though you are pregnant in the workplace. For many patients this is the same emotionally, as a transfer will mean the chance and hope for a child. Medically, people may vary in their response, but to many patients transfer means potential pregnancy or actual pregnancy.

If there is a negative pregnancy test following transfer, how do people cope with this?

Again, there is no standard way to deal with this but in general it is an incredibly hard thing to go through and many people feel it is a grieving experience. There is a huge potential for loss and the fear that this may never happen, while needing somehow to find a way forward (either carrying on with more treatment or looking to alternatives), and all of this, combined with the comedown from all the hormones, can be a painful mix.

People often take time out to grieve a little and to step off the treadmill, but other people will prefer to keep on going almost immediately to cope with the pain. There is no right way forward – it is just essential to be kind to oneself.

What are the biggest misconceptions about IVF?

Where do I begin! That it's a woman's problem, that it's the fault of career-focused women, that it's a situation solved by relaxing more/trusting God more/being a better person. That people going through IVF are selfish and should 'just' adopt. There are far too many false assumptions, but fertility treatment exists because of a need for medical help for a problem around reproduction.

What are the biggest obstacles and challenges families must deal with post-loss (following IVF)?

All loss is devastating, and loss following treatment has additional complexities to be faced.

Not only are they dealing with the grief of losing their longed-for child, they are also dealing with the physical issues, which include huge hormone variations over several months following treatment. They may also need to come to terms with the fact that to try for another child, they need to start the whole treatment process all over again (if that is even possible due to finances, health, etc.).

Loss after treatment brings home the vulnerability of IVF – it is an amazing science but in no way guarantees a child at the end of the process.

What is your best advice for someone considering IVF for the first time?

Get prepared, do the research and be incredibly kind to yourself. Infertility is a huge issue to deal with and around 90 per cent of people will experience problems with depression at some point. IVF doesn't take all this away; it provides a medical route forward, but it is a difficult one physically, mentally and emotionally, and it will take its toll in the process.

There is some amazing support out there (see pages 382–4), so find the people who will help you through, and create a good support structure. Take some time to plan and think carefully about who and what will help you through this stage in life. Don't underestimate what you are taking on and be your own best friend throughout.

What is your best advice for family and friends on how to support someone who is having IVF?

Ask them how you can help and what they need and be prepared for the long haul. It can be an incredibly lonely and long process and you will need to guard against compassion fatigue if supporting someone long term. A good friend or family member really can make a huge difference, though, so do ask specifically what 'good support' means and looks like to the person you are supporting!

What are your best tips for making IVF an easier process?

Realising the enormity of what you are doing and then getting equipped in any way you know will help. This will vary from person to person, so take time to build a plan and support structure. Keep as busy as works for you. For some, keeping active is a wonderful distraction; while others will need to slow down and simplify. You will know ultimately what works best, so make a plan and implement it as a priority.

Any other advice or tips?

If you can see IVF as a course of treatment rather than a one-off event, it will help, as it often takes time to be successful, if at all.

Flexibility, perseverance and self-compassion would be my top recommendations!

✳✳✳✳✳✳✳✳✳✳✳✳✳✳✳✳✳✳✳✳✳✳✳✳

3

Practical Considerations

PLANNING A FUNERAL

Funerals are often planned in a fog of grief and it is so hard even to know where to start. Firstly, let me tell you this: whatever the gestation of your baby, you can have a funeral. Often people assume their baby needs to be of a certain age, but this is untrue. So, if you want a funeral for your baby, you can have one. Many choose to have no service or funeral at all and that is also okay, but this section is aimed at those who do want to plan a funeral.

If your loss took place in a hospital setting, they may offer to handle the funeral, which is often a group cremation (many babies being cremated together) and a group service (for all the families of those babies). Some people prefer this option as it means they don't need to take on the planning of the event; for others, it feels too impersonal and they prefer to arrange things themselves. Many funeral directors offer a free service for babies, so do ask about a complimentary service before booking a particular company.

If your baby is in the hospital mortuary, they will keep your child there until the funeral directors take him or her to their premises. Once you have booked the funeral directors, they will guide you through the process of what to do next.

Some people choose to have both a cremation or burial and a separate service of remembrance. Often these are on the same day, so everyone gathers for the service of remembrance, and then close family and friends move on to the burial or cremation. However, some prefer to have only one service, and others like to have two but a week apart. All of this is your choice, and you can dictate how you want the order of events to go.

Most parents will tell you their big fear is holding an event to say goodbye to their baby and no one showing up. I urge you to fight this fear and plan what you want for your little one, as the only truly important people attending are you (and your partner if you have one). Others say to me they are worried that people may feel they are creating too much fuss (especially for babies lost at a very young gestation). Again, I say to you, it doesn't matter what others think – this is YOUR BABY, YOUR CHILD, and no one should rob you of the chance to say a formal goodbye if that is what you want.

Are funeral cars needed? Some people say absolutely yes, others feel they aren't required. In fact, for some people having their baby in their car feels right, so just take time to think about what you want for you and your family.

Flowers? Again, this is such a personal decision. Some people opt for flowers from the immediate family and then ask for donations to a charity. The Mariposa Trust, for instance, depends on people kindly donating like this, and every time a family makes a donation in honour of their lost baby, it helps another family get vital support.

What should you include in the service? The answer to this is anything you want; make it as personal as you like. Music, poetry, personal letters you have written to your child. To see a sample service sheet, please go to www.sayinggoodbye.org

Where does the baby get buried? Again, this is a truly personal decision. Some people want the baby buried with relatives who have passed away; others want them as close to their home as possible.

I always advise people to visit different sites, and find the one that they feel is right for their baby to rest in.

A few key tips:

If you are including in the service photos or videos of babies that have passed, be aware that some people have never seen a dead body, and while this is your much-loved baby, and a sight of utter beauty, people can react strangely to seeing any dead person. I often advise just including pictures of hands and feet if people are unsure, or using black and white photos, as this means colour variants (which can be what shocks people the most) aren't really noticeable.

Make it clear to people if you would like them to attend the service. I hear from many people who would have loved to attend the funeral of their niece or nephew but they presumed it was a parent-only event, and they didn't want to intrude – so if you want people to attend, be clear about it and explain why it would mean a lot to you.

Have things planned for the days that follow the funeral. Allow friends or family to visit, for instance. Often people have a big dip in emotion after the funeral: they tend to be on autopilot while they have an event to occupy them, but once it is over what do they focus on next? Some people go away for a few days, others don't want to stray far from home (as they often feel more secure in their home environment), but it helps to have plans for the 5–7 days after the funeral – even if it's just having coffee with a friend each day. (Any family and friends who are reading this, please be aware of this post-funeral dip and rally around. So much support vanishes after this event, and it's often when people need it the most.)

Fear Post-Loss

One of the legacies of loss that is so rarely discussed is the fear that remains even when you are physically recovered. This is especially the case for those who have suffered recurrent loss. If you have had to endure a period of time in fear, constantly waiting for the bottom to fall from your world, your body gets used to operating on a fight-or-flight response. Your stress hormones, adrenaline and cortisol, are always pumping, and your brain is waiting for you to face the worst-case scenario. Even if you are blessed to then have a baby in your arms, it is super-hard to switch off this response, and it can take years to master controlling it, but sadly most people just learn to live with it rather than stopping it.

Those who have lost a baby but are blessed to have a child to raise will tell you that once you have lost a child you become hyper-protective of the ones you have here with you. At times this overprotectiveness can look like a person is paranoid, sensing disaster at every turn. For example, a person behaving 100 per cent rationally would see a seagull sitting next to their child as a sweet photo opportunity. A mother who lives with this constant fear will see that seagull as a vulture, with the potential to peck their little one's eyes out, and possibly carry their child away! While I can laugh at myself and find humour in being able to twist an innocent moment into a potentially dangerous situation, I constantly fight this fear, and have to choose not to be too overprotective, but it's not easy. We all need to accept that our natural response is to want to wrap our children in cotton wool, but as we want them to have a wonderful childhood, without carrying false fear, we should take a step backwards and ask: is this really dangerous, or is this just life and part of childhood?

Post-loss fear is so terribly hard to live with, and choosing to trade in that fear, and hold on to hope, will really help you move forwards. If you give in to it, it can slowly take hold of so many other areas of life, so it is essential to silence the mind and refuse to allow it to capitalise on every little worry. A few common fear areas which people often struggle with post-loss include:

Fear of illness for yourself or others

This can be overwhelming and all-consuming. It can be concerns over little things or big things, and every symptom is overanalysed. When a person's imagination gets involved, even a common cold can look like a life-threatening condition.

I can't even begin to tell you how horrible this is for those who suffer with this fear, as it truly robs life of all joy. I always recommend people to have counselling or cognitive behavioural therapy (CBT) if they are suffering with this, as the quicker this pattern of thinking is stopped, the better. Being crippled by the fear of illness can be as bad as actually having the illness they fear.

Fear of accidents

This is another fear where the imagination can take you to some very dark places. Someone tells you they are just popping to the shops and will be back in 30 minutes. However, in that time you have already imagined they have been involved in a head-on collision and you are sitting waiting for the police to knock on your door to break the bad news to you.

There are some key skills to stop this cycle of thinking and the main one is to nip the negative thought in the bud the moment it rears its head.

Don't allow yourself to even enter into the dialogue in your brain. So the second you think 'what if', choose to think of something completely different. Once you start down the path of the accident, you are engaged in the thought pattern, so divert the thought, think of anything but – for example, what shall we have for supper? What would Lisa like for Christmas? You need to do a 180-degree turn; eventually the negative thoughts should stop surfacing. If they don't, consider having some counselling.

Fear of bad news

This is very similar to fearing accidents and the same applies. Nip negative thoughts in the bud and don't engage with this spiral of fear.

Fear of going out

Sadly, this is quite common post-loss. Home can quickly become a safe place, somewhere a person feels they can be real and authentic, and the world outside can seem scary and fast-paced.

While it's fine to take time out and to hide away in our homes, we need to be careful that we don't avoid going out for too long, as this fear can really sneak up on you from nowhere. I always recommend simply going for short walks or brief drives regularly, so you at least see outside of your front door, and this can help avoid agoraphobia creeping in the back door.

Fear of socialising

This may start because a person has been in a situation where someone has said something painful to them, or it may start because they fear that they can't be real or authentic to themselves or their pain in the presence of other people. Either way, it's another fear that's better to fight early on, as the last thing you want is to become a recluse if you have previously loved being with people and socialising.

I suggest you start gently and spend time with those most likely to be sensitive and kind, then slowly expand your social circle. Remember, it is okay to realise certain people were never really your friend, or a kind person. I call grief 'the great revealer'; it's like a massive sieve and it brings so many issues and realities to the surface, and a common thing post-loss is finding out that some people aren't as lovely as you thought they were. So be mindful of this, especially if that has prompted your fear of socialising to develop. If your fear does continue, counselling can really help.

Fear of blood loss

Periods. Monthly bleeding. The time of the month. Auntie's flow. It has many names, and, for some reason, it's a taboo topic. Post-baby loss, especially miscarriage (including ectopic and molar pregnancies), periods can be traumatising to women, particularly for any woman who has suffered any form of post-traumatic stress due to their loss (or how their loss was managed.)

So how can this manifest itself? Well, the moment they see blood (even though they are no longer pregnant), a wave of feelings and emotions can hit them like a tidal wave. They can feel panic, fear, their heart may race and they may feel consumed by terror, and it can take hours or even days for their peace to return. The blood has become a trigger, you see, and just the sight of it takes the person back to that time in their life where blood was associated with their baby passing.

How can we help people who feel this way?

Firstly, we can acknowledge there is a recognised problem and reassure them it is totally understandable to feel the way they do. Just by doing this it can help people, as it stops them feeling alone, and it also removes the shame and embarrassment.

Secondly, we can encourage them to get help. By reaching out to a charity (such as the Mariposa Trust – www.sayinggoodbye.org), or to their GP or to a counsellor, help can be provided. Often people just need to be taught coping strategies so that when a trigger happens, symptoms can be controlled and managed.

Most importantly, people need to know this is a hugely common issue following a baby loss, and it in no way means they 'are losing it' (which is what people ask me constantly). This is just a hard part of recovering mentally post-loss, and simply by knowing you are not alone in your feelings, it can truly help. I beg you not to remain walking in fear, however that terror manifests itself; there is help available. It is possible to fight all fear and deal with it, even if that inner voice is yelling at you that it's not possible. Walking through life carrying this burden is truly debilitating – it is like having chains wrapped around your ankles. It shackles you, and I want you to be free!

The Mariposa Trust surveyed 366 people about blood-loss fear: 20.82 per cent of people suffered with panic and fear when using the loo post-loss (this equates to over one in five).

So, if you have this fear you are not alone!

Intimacy Following Loss

As you will be able to appreciate, this is an extremely tricky subject to tackle, as not only does the type of loss you have encountered play a part in the resuming of intimacy, personality and your relationship with your partner also affect a person's response and feelings about re-engaging at an intimate level. What I can say is nothing and no one should force you into any physical intimacy before you feel ready and willing.

Perhaps a good place to start with this conversation is to talk about hugging and holding hands. For some, they need this physical touch to feel loved and cared for; for others, they don't want any physical contact, as they feel safer being in a bubble. This is something that needs to be discussed between partners (also with families and friends who may want to hug you), to ensure everyone's needs and expectations are being met. Where it becomes difficult in all areas of intimacy (whether it be basic physical touch or sexual intimacy) is when one partner feels one way, and the other feels very differently. What can you do if one party feels a need to have sex to feel loved and cared for, but the other can't even cope with the thought of it? The only answer to this is to talk about it. Not in order for one party to convince the other to do what they want, but so all feelings can be expressed and heard, as it's important to understand what page each person is on. Over time, and with much discussion, there is a chance that both people may feel a similar way. If, however, it becomes an 'issue', and a marriage/relationship is in danger because of it, I would always suggest seeing a counsellor, as having a third party involved with the discussion can help bring greater understanding and clarity.

So when is it okay to resume sexual activity? This 100 per cent depends on the type of loss you have had, and you need to be guided by your doctor. A general rule is no sex until all bleeding has finished, in a bid to avoid infection, but you really do need to be advised by a medical professional, as the last thing you want is to encounter medical issues in addition to your loss. Once you re-engage with sexual intimacy, you should ensure you use contraception, unless you want to risk conceiving again quickly.

Sex post-loss can be truly difficult, especially if sex has become more about creating a child (which can often be the case if a person has either struggled to conceive, or has had multiple loss). To re-engage with sexual activity can bring a whole new wave of grief, and an overwhelming feeling of being back at square one can consume you. With this in mind, expect tears and be willing to talk about and share your feelings. I always suggest to people who fear intimacy post-loss to start slowly – imagine you are going back to the dating stage of your relationship. It can sometimes even be good to take sex out of the equation, and say no sex at all for x amount of time. This can be really helpful to some people, and knowing there is going to be nothing more on offer than a kiss and a hug can remove all pressure.

Of course, there will be others who want to have sex and intimacy as quickly as possible, and that too is totally understandable. I know people who have said the sex they had post-loss was the best they'd ever had, as there was an intimacy there that they had never experienced before. When you feel at one with your partner, it can make the pain you are feeling emotionally shared, and this can make you feel less alone in your suffering.

Often people start having sex again to try for another baby, and that is totally okay. Having another child does not mean you are trying to replace the one you have lost. No child is replaceable, and it is 100 per cent natural to want to have another baby post-loss. And you need to let go of any guilt you may have – you are purely wanting to give the child you lost a sibling, remember that.

We made the decision to try again for another child straight away after most of our losses. We didn't want to take time to recover emotionally; we decided we would rather recover while trying for another baby. Others, though, prefer to wait until they are stronger emotionally/mentally – both options are fine.

A lot of people feel they don't want to try again until they can mentally handle another loss, and that is fine, but I always caution that for some that day may never come. I know I would have always said I can't face or cope with another loss, and I think most people will feel that way. I was also conscious that the longer I waited, the greater the fear grew. In the end I simply had to say I will never be okay with losing another baby; however, my yearning for a child is so great, I have to just jump in the deep end and hope for the best. For others, this would be the wrong approach and they need to wait until they feel much stronger. Only you know you. So trust your instincts and go with what you feel is right.

If sex has become hard work and only about baby making, I really encourage you to talk, and to try to mix it up a bit. Try not to focus on 'fertile days' or treat sex as a means to an end. Remember, it is a way of connecting with your partner, and only you can ensure the passion and excitement remain in the relationship. It is so easy to read the many helpful (and many unhelpful) tips on how to conceive fast, and before you know it sex becomes a prescribed physical and biology experiment. While it may be true that you have a better chance of conceiving if you have sex at x time, in x position and then sit with your legs up a wall for 30 minutes while eating marshmallows, if you only do this, sex can become tiresome for anyone. (PS: I added in the [ironic] marshmallows to show the things we are willing to try. I have never heard that marshmallow-eating helps conception, but it would be a nice thing to eat, I am sure, and if someone now tries it and it works, let me know!)

My top tips:

* Talk to your partner
* Take medical advice on when it is okay to resume sexual intimacy
* Take it a step at a time and don't let anyone rush you
* Don't be afraid to show emotion (intimacy post-loss is ALWAYS super-emotional)

The Mariposa Trust asked 250 people about intimacy post-loss. The make-up of this group was 98% female and 2% male.

How quickly post-loss did you return to physical intimacy?
Immediately 14.8%; 4–6 weeks 38%; 6–12 weeks 22%; 12+ weeks 23.6%; never 1.6%

Who instigated physical intimacy for the first time post-loss?
You 23.29%; partner 32.13%; both 42.57%; N/A 2.01%

Did you initially enjoy intimacy post-loss?
Yes 36%; no 61.2%; N/A 2.8%

Did you engage in physical intimacy in order to try for another baby or for another reason?
Yes, we were trying for a baby 36.03%; for fun 4.86%; for connection 59.11%

Did you want physical intimacy (post-loss) or were you just doing it to please/satisfy your partner?
Yes, I wanted intimacy 59.44%; I was doing it for my partner 31.73%; N/A 8.84%

Were you scared of having physical intimacy post-loss?
Yes 74.8%; no 25.2%

Did physical intimacy become solely about having more children post-loss?
Yes 38.4%; no 58%; N/A 3.6%

Martin's Story

From my first date with Susi I have never struggled to express my love and affection, holding hands, even kissing in public. It has always been something I've enjoyed more than anything. Being with Susi made me feel complete, excited, and, to borrow clichés from the worst of romance novelists, those early days of our relationship were charged with an electric intimacy.

A year into our relationship, we experienced two miscarriages in what was, looking back, an incredibly short space of time. Anyone who goes through a similar loss will probably tell you that at the time every day feels a very long time. With the sadness of loss, the intimacy that we shared changed, the exciting rush, the tingling intensity developed into something deeper. Where before it had been an exciting, sensation-charged intimacy, a deeper, more protective dimension developed. Perhaps it was a reaction to the less than kind words of both sets of parents; my own mother's cruel words that there must be something wrong with Susi, or her own mother's words that perhaps it was for the better rather than tell her father.

Within the year, we were married, had moved to a new house and were blessed with the birth of our daughter. All within the space of a couple of months. Throughout this often-stressful time, the intimacy of our love was something that made our relationship stronger. I haven't really realised or acknowledged that the feeling of a need to protect Susi has been there ever since. I still get that rush of excitement, that feeling in my chest whenever we're together, but it's a lot deeper and more mature than it was for that same guy 17 years ago.

Susi's Story

I have never struggled with being close with my husband. We are very 'touchy-feely', hugging, always holding hands, and have never struggled with public displays of affection. And I have loved him deeply since the moment we met.

After losing our two babies in a short space of time, I found that the intimacy between us changed and it was like a rollercoaster for me.

I found that my emotions were all over the place; we were closer than ever after each loss, but, also, I found that I was closing myself down (self-preservation in my eyes). My husband was kind, gentle and loving and giving constant support emotionally. We would cuddle together at night, but I would feel that I wasn't ready to go any further than that for what felt like quite a while. I just wanted to be held. Intimacy changed; for me, it was filled with fear – one of the most important parts of our marriage, where I felt the most loved and felt like we were one, was now marred with the pain of loss. The loss of two children who I hadn't carried to full term fell heavy on me.

My husband was so loving and patient and would hold me close every minute he could, and he made me feel safe, helping me slowly overcome the fear of loss again.

We were very blessed a year later to have a beautiful baby girl. We will never forget those times of loss, but we have grown together through this and I believe it has made us stronger. Being gentle with each other, taking our time and showing love is what helped me through this time. Take time for each other, it really works.

Claire's Story

So then. Sex after miscarriage. Other than the obvious 'Will it hurt?' or 'Will my vagina fall out?' or, even, 'What if they left a speculum up there?', I was pretty trusting of the medical professionals when they told me that sex would be okay. I admit it was a worrying and confusing time – we had had two straightforward-ish births before and I had never once considered miscarriage could happen to me, but mingled with all of this was a sense that I needed to be pregnant again and it needed to be as soon as possible.

I don't know who I needed to prove it to, but the six weeks after that first miscarriage were long and, as soon as we were able to have sex again, we were off. My poor husband had to endure a wife who would suddenly give him her best seductive smile (not bothering to check first for basil in her teeth) and who would dig at the bottom of the wardrobe for some sexy lingerie. After the first miscarriage I was blessed to get pregnant quickly (the sexy lingerie got placed back at the bottom of the wardrobe) and nine months later my precious third son arrived. However, after the second and third miscarriages things became way more complicated. In fact, the third was actually an ectopic pregnancy and, until the pain and bleeding began, I hadn't even known I was pregnant.

Picture the scene: the day before our tenth wedding anniversary I was meant to be packing for a romantic weekend away in the Lake District. A boutique room with a four-poster bed, a hot tub and a beautiful bathroom with fancy lighting was ours for two whole nights. Pure bliss. Except that the day before our tenth wedding anniversary I was actually crying in pain at the doctor's, dreading the moment he would pack me off to the hospital, shattering my hopes of romance, relaxation and – more importantly – uninterrupted sleep! It was devastating to us. A few hours later and, yes, at the hospital – after scans and blood tests and urine samples – I was told that I would be allowed to go but with certain instructions: 1 – that we would go to the nearest hospital if anything untoward suddenly happened (no endless bottles of champagne in the hot tub then); 2 – I had to take it easy (shame we were next door to a fancy spa then); 3 – we would abstain from sex (probably for the best; I mean, with all those rose petals on the bed, surely it would be too uncomfortable anyway?). All in all, I was so relieved to be actually allowed to go that I accepted the conditions without a second thought. Our romantic get-away was perfect . . . mostly.

I tried to forget the fact I was bleeding, crying at the tiniest of things, and that I wriggled constantly throughout my facial with a dodgy-sounding Swedish woman because I needed yet another wee really badly. But the fact remained that we had lost another little life and nothing could gloss over the sadness that we felt. Sex after miscarriage was not something we took lightly, but I am glad we didn't wait too long before (ahem) 'jumping back on the horse' again.

(Sorry about that.) And as we approach our 20th wedding anniversary in a few years, I can only hope there will be a romantic getaway with uninterrupted passion, champagne and fancy bathroom lighting. But no sexy lingerie – that's been promoted to the best dusting cloth in the house.

Heidi's Story

After our losses (my first and second pregnancies) I was desperate to just get pregnant again. I couldn't bear seeing all these happy pregnant people, posting their bump pics online, having baby showers and buying all the gear. It should have been me, that should be my happiness, but mine got stolen from me in the cruelest of ways through no fault of my own and I thought, if I can just get pregnant again, it'll make it better.

Therefore sex became a chore, a means to an end. My body had let me down; my body didn't do what a woman's body is supposed to do. I had lots of medical intervention with my losses. I had been prodded and poked; things had been shoved up inside of me; strangers, some men, opening my legs to see what was happening while blood was pouring out of me; been put under general anesthetic; and had multiple operations where, again, strangers went up inside of me while I was knocked out. I felt traumatised, humiliated, like a piece of meat or a science project to be messed with because my body had got it all wrong. I found that baby loss is physically gross, degrading and emotionally agonising.

Afterwards I did not feel at all sexy; I didn't feel confident, secure and proud in my own skin. I wished I could just take a pill and be pregnant again; sex was literally the *last* thing I felt like doing, but the only way to get pregnant again was to have sex. On top of all of this, my husband and I were often grieving in different ways and at different times, and this put a huge strain on our marriage. Making love to him for pleasure was not high on my agenda.

I knew my dates of ovulation; in fact, I think I even put them in my diary. There was no romance, no spontaneity; it was just a job I had to get done to try to get a live baby in my arms as quickly as possible. I had to pretend to my husband that I wanted it. I remember thinking, 'Okay, you have to do it tonight, so game face on.' My husband did not want to have sex if I didn't want it, as it 'felt so wrong'. In hindsight, this was kindness and love, but at the time I wanted to rage at him. But I had a two-night window to get the job done, so I just lied and pretended that I wanted it so he'd just get on and do it.

I remember once he felt under so much pressure that he couldn't climax. It caused a big argument where I shouted, 'You literally have one job to do!' The whole thing was awful. I felt so ashamed. Ashamed that I was going about sex in this way, ashamed that I was pretending and there-fore lying to my husband, and mortified that even when I put on my best 'performance' he couldn't get the job done. It was too embarrassing to talk to anyone about this; I felt so frustrated, angry and sad. Not only did my baby die, I had to go through the physical torment of losing my baby, my marriage was under strain, most of my friends were pregnant or with newborns and I just couldn't face them, and now I felt like I was losing my mind! I *never* wanted to become this woman. I'd heard of women having sex just to get pregnant and I remember thinking that it was ridiculous. I always thought that I was going to make my baby out of love; it was going to be exciting and fun. Losing a baby does something to your mind; it affects your mental health. Grief is *the* biggest turn-off, but sex is the only way to get what you so desperately want. It's a lose–lose, crappy situation. Every month when I took the test and I still wasn't pregnant, I used to think, 'All that for nothing.'

(I want to add here, sex did finally pay off in the end, and today I am writing this with my toddler sitting at my feet.)

Jane's Story

We never struggled with intimacy; a delicate stroke as we passed each other, holding hands when out, snuggles on the sofa and spooning to sleep. It always felt natural and the goose-pimple tingles were ever-present.

After we lost our little rose, the intimacy stayed, but it changed. It was caring, tender, supportive, providing comfort. It was not exciting or tingly; those times had gone. Not having that pressure was what I needed, and it was assumed, not asked for. I was grateful for that.

We were initially advised against having another baby, but this changed at a later consultation and I remember that sinking feeling of how were we going to be that couple again. I wanted another baby so much, but it was important that we moved forwards as a couple and that the desire to get pregnant did not dictate or change our previously loving relationship.

I think the one thing that worried me the most was that things would feel different. That the sympathy would be evident. It was not. The journey of loss had been travelled by us both, and while that understandably changed us as a couple, for ever, it did not change who we were and what brought us together in the first place. It had always felt natural, being perfectly together, and that remained. The most important lesson I learnt was to not put too much pressure on myself and to try not to overthink the situation. We now have a healthy and happy four-year-old and our relationship is stronger than ever. And the goose pimples are back.

Returning to Work

Returning to work after loss can be petrifying. It's a daunting thing to do after the loss of any loved one. Loss changes you, yet when people return to work they are often expected to be their old selves, which can be challenging.

Some people are entitled to paid bereavement leave, whereas others aren't even entitled to a single day of paid leave, and this is another huge challenge with baby loss. People need time to recover both physically and emotionally, and only you know how much time you feel you need or want to take off work. If you aren't automatically given bereavement leave but you need time off, please book an appointment with your doctor. While they can't force your employer to pay you for time off, they can give you a doctor's sick note. Sometimes doctors write down depression as the reason for needing time off, and I often hear from people who resent this, as they so rightly tell me, 'But, Zoë, I am not depressed, I am grieving and there is a big difference.' Sadly, however, many doctors won't or can't list grief as a reason for time off work, so depression is often cited instead. The important thing here is that you have the space to recover emotionally, so if you are able financially to take time off, do consider it.

A note for the self-employed: I know this advice will come down to finances, and whether your work and clients will wait for you to return to work – sometimes jobs don't allow for any leave, and that is just something that has to be accepted – but if you can take time off, please do. Be a kind boss to yourself, and force yourself to look after your physical and emotional needs.

The Mariposa Trust asked 198 people about their experience with employers following baby loss, and these are the results:

* 79.9% of people were given time off after losing their baby.
* 57.73% of people were given time specifically to grieve.
* 35.23% of people felt their physical or mental health suffered due to a lack of support by their employer.
* 16.06% of people felt that they lost their job or promotional prospects due to losing a baby.

A few practical tips for returning to work:

* Prepare in your mind what you will say to work colleagues about your loss. Just having a set answer can help you deal with that unexpected conversation in the office car park.
* Try to return on a part-time basis – perhaps mornings only, or three full days – even if this is just for the first

few days or weeks. A tiered return can help with the adjustment into normal life.

* Don't be surprised if you feel physically exhausted when you return to work. Keeping in control of your emotions is physically taxing, so add this to the daily physical tasks of your job, it makes sense why you may feel so drained. Ensure you have as many breaks as you are able to take. If you can take time to go for a walk, or just outside in the fresh air, do it. Take your lunch break and coffee breaks, even if you normally just power through – your mind and body will need these times to regroup.

* For the first few weeks following your return to work don't make evening plans; use your evenings to relax and process your thoughts and, importantly, to sleep. The world can quickly feel overstimulating, and you need to give your mind time each day to chill out.

* Eat healthily. The right foods can help you regain your strength and it is important to eat a balanced and healthy diet post-loss. Iron-rich produce and foods that maintain your blood glucose levels will all help you feel more emotionally stable.

* Explain to your employer that on returning you may need more support, and to be met with weeks or months of backdated work will not help you perform well.

The crucial thing to be aware of is that it will be hard to return to work, and the last thing you need is to be overwhelmed with work on your first week back. Be gentle with yourself and ask your employer to be thoughtful too.

Cassie's Story

As a neonatal nurse, I love my job. It's exciting, and intense, heartbreaking at times and yet so completely fantastic when you get to see these tiny, poorly babies overcome huge hurdles to go home with their parents. Before becoming a parent, I felt I had compassion and empathy. I felt I supported my families through the hard times. I also felt I could deal with any situation, confidently and appropriately. Then we had our daughter. She was born extremely prematurely and she died within a few hours of her birth. She was with us, in our arms. From huge excitement about being a mummy came the devastation of our loss. We had 24 hours of kindness before going home, my arms empty, to the nothingness that awaited us at home. Going back to the job I loved filled me with absolute dread. Surely, every baby would remind me of mine. How could I be that confident nurse again? But, every baby wasn't mine, they belonged to other desperate parents, fighting their battles with them. And I could see their fight, so raw and pure. And I had so much more insight into how I could help them. And those poor families that lose their precious babies. I could speak from the heart about the road ahead, and tell them that while it feels like you'll never make it, one day you will remember your baby with so much love and pride and it will shape the caring and strong person you will become, because of them. I miss our daughter so much, and am often reminded of her at work, but she makes me a much stronger and better version of who I used to be.

Rachel's Story

Returning to work after my first miscarriage was difficult, although my line manager had been very supportive throughout. She suggested a gradual return as she understood that I wouldn't be quite up to a full day's work, so this was very welcome. I felt like taking another week off to recover was too much as we were quite busy at work, plus I felt the routine might help me to stop constantly thinking about it all.

When the day came, I was incredibly nervous, and felt sick, worrying about how I would cope with people asking how I was, having been away for a week, then about if I had enough products with me for the blood loss I was still dealing with and did I need to take spare clothing just in case.

When I got to the office it was awkward, no one quite knew what to say; a few people I worked with directly asked if I was okay and said they were very sorry. I just nodded to them in reply, I just couldn't say anything. I visited the toilet several times to have a quick cry throughout the day.

A few days in, a colleague came up to me, gave me a hug and said she had suffered a stillbirth several years ago, she understood how I was feeling and if I wanted to talk she was there for me. I was amazed how open she was. I felt like I was carrying this awful secret beforehand but suddenly I felt like I wasn't going through it alone. She wasn't the only one either – a few weeks later, another colleague said she'd suffered a few losses and again she was there if I needed her.

This helped me through it and after a few more weeks I was worrying less about what people would think of me and was able to be more open about it.

Amy's Story

Returning to work for me after loss was like walking in a daze where externally you look okay but internally are shattered.

I sat in meetings planning events which I never would have been at had my baby lived. Trying to carry on with office banter while part of me had died. Then there are the pregnancy announcements of colleagues who are due when you were. If they know about your loss they generally avoid you, and if not, you try to be enthusiastic while wondering why you couldn't keep yours. I remember going to the toilets to cry, as that was the only place I could take five minutes and you can't control when the grief wave hits. However, work for me was also a reminder that life goes on, a perspective shift, an environment where friends distract you and help the pain lessen. When my rainbow baby was due, it helped me focus on not dwelling in fear.

Helen's Story

When I finally was ready to return to work after losing my baby, I realised I was going to have to face another unplanned hurdle. I hadn't told anyone I was pregnant before I had lost my baby. The doctor had signed me off with 'stress'. No one on my mainly female team knew and I was unprepared for how to deal with it all. I was barely functioning, silently and actively grieving and scared that if anyone asked me if I was okay I would crumple to the floor. The first day back, I avoided everyone as much as possible, tried to keep my head down and get on with it, but it just didn't work. Within an hour I was in the loo, in floods of tears and desperate to go home. My boss found me and I blurted it all out. She found a quiet room, listened to me and sent me home. Over the next few days I worked shorter hours and gradually took my full-time role back on again.

Fast-forward a few months and I again had a miscarriage, the second in a sequence of recurrent losses. I knew that after the first experience of returning to work I had to do things a different way and take control of this situation. Before I returned to work, I contacted my boss and asked her to tell the team why I had been off work, but to respect that I didn't want to discuss it on my return. This totally took the fear element out of returning. Knowing that I wasn't going to be asked an awkward question was a massive relief. I also planned a soft return, working on a project that meant I could work from home if I didn't feel like facing the office but still getting me back into the swing of things and helping me start 'ordinary' life again. Gaining that element of power back into my life was a real comfort, especially at a time when things felt so chaotic and missing.

Social Media

Many people will tell you that they have a love–hate relationship with social media at the best of times, let alone when they are going through any traumatic or life-changing experience. My personal belief is that it can be a great tool for disseminating news and expressing feelings one may be experiencing, and it can also play a key role in bringing like-minded people together. That said, I am also acutely aware that it can make some feel very alone and judged.

The problem with social media is that if a person is seen to share 'too much' personal information they may be judged as attention-seeking. On the flipside, if a person does not share enough honest feelings, others may assume they are emotionally fine and much-needed support may not then be forthcoming. So, what is the right balance? This is something only you can determine and a lot will depend on who you are connected with on social media. If it is just family and close friends, you may feel social media is a good way to communicate your news; if you have a much wider social-media audience, you may want to be a lot more selective.

Choose whether you want to make a statement about your loss on social media. Some people want to post one message and not have to keep sharing the news, and, if you feel like this, a notice on social-media platforms may be a good option for you. Sayinggoodbye.org offers pre-made images which you can just download and share, so you may want to explore that option. Before you post your message, consider the audience, and also be clear on what you want the response to be from those who read it, maybe by including this in your post – for example, 'while we greatly value your support we would appreciate no calls for the next few days'. Practical guidance can help friends and family understand how best to respond.

Be aware that some respond on social media without properly engaging their brains, so at times people may post insensitive comments and responses. It is really hard to gauge people's intention and emotion on social media, so try to read comments and remarks with eyes of grace, and choose to think the best of people, rather than immediately taking offence. I understand this is easy to write and hard to do, but the last thing you need right now is to be carrying feelings of resentment.

If you want to keep people informed on social media but you don't feel emotionally capable, ask your partner, a friend or a family member to look after your accounts for a few days or weeks. They can then post your messages and respond to comments (and also delete any comments that they think you may not appreciate). Consider starting a group chat, where you can post one message to a select few family members or friends; it can be so much easier to post one message to 10 people, rather than saying the same thing over and over again.

Be aware that forums and chat rooms may not be a helpful environment for everyone. In my experience, forums and chat rooms can often bring together a lot of people who are hurting, and they can make people feel quickly lost, scared and fearing the future. Of course, there will be the exception and you may stumble across some like-minded new friends, but I always suggest one-to-one support is a lot healthier and more personal.

Follow supportive social-media accounts and pages – the Saying Goodbye Facebook page, my Instagram and Pinterest accounts upload daily support and quotes, and they can help people feel less alone and more understood. By sharing posts from these pages, you can also let your friends and family know how you are feeling without having to find your own words.

My top tips:

* Be cautious what you post.
* Try not to be offended if people don't respond in the way you would like, or if they don't respond at all.
* If you want specific people to know your news, ensure they do know by sending them a personal message, as it's easy to miss posts on social media, and some people who are especially close to you may feel offended to hear news about loss on social media at the same time as everyone else.
* Only you know whether this is the right place to share your precious photos and images, but if you do share photos of any baby or child that has passed away always post a warning so people can emotionally prepare themselves before seeing the photo.
* Be prepared for people to tag you in on any story or news they see on loss. It is often people's way of showing you

they still remember what you went through.

* Most social-media platforms now allow you to mute or unfollow people's daily news and posts, and you may want to consider doing this with certain people. If hearing about a person's baby not sleeping is going to bring you any feelings of hurt or frustration, choose not to look at it; it won't help you, or help your relationship with them, so just mute their news feed (on Instagram) or unfollow their news (on Facebook). They won't ever know you have done it since you still remain as a friend and follower.

* Try not to compare your grief or your story with other people's. Social media is a hothouse for this and comparing your walk through grief with another's isn't helpful or healthy. This is your walk – so, yes, be encouraged by people and use social media to feel less alone, but if someone's posts are making you feel more isolated or causing you additional pain, don't torture yourself by reading them.

Esther's Story

When I first fell pregnant, Facebook had just become 'a thing' and Twitter wasn't far behind. I loved Facebook; I kept in touch with friends and family and I still find social media a great tool of communication and support. When I had my first child, I eagerly awaited the moment to announce it on social media. With our first we waited until 12 weeks. We loved thinking how we would announce it – we knew it would surprise people as it had surprised us!

As most parents do, we loved sharing on social media photos of our daughter growing up; long-distance relatives loved it too. I often updated on all aspects of my life as I am open as a person, but I also loved that social media connected me with so many friends; as an extrovert, I loved being able to share the fun, as well as the mundane and tough parts of my life, with those who cared and would 'listen'. It wasn't fake; I was careful with my friends list and I wanted it to be 'real', reflecting my day-to-day reality online.

Then I fell pregnant again. We didn't want to wait to announce as we had with our first because we were so excited and a baby is a baby at whatever time in the womb. So we shared our news. Everyone congratulated us and we were so excited. Then I started to bleed. We went for a check-up and everything was good, there was a strong heartbeat. But by 11 weeks I was bleeding again and this time there was no heartbeat.

How would I come to terms with my loss and let the whole online world know too? I couldn't just not say anything, everyone had congratulated me; so I decided to share it on social media as a therapeutic process, but also to give my baby a story, her story, that was read by my friends and those who cared from afar online.

I logged in to tell the world about my heartbreak and give my baby a name and a purpose, but there I saw a perfect scan photo and our good friends announcing the 12-week scan of their second baby. This was the first we had known and the due date was the exact date of my baby. It was the most agonising thing to see in the depths of my grief.

What to do? I congratulated them and then I went offline. Social media can be so cold when you get struck by someone's update without any context to their feelings, your feelings and the whole situation. It needs relationships too. Social media is often 2D, it doesn't show empathy; it just throws out the good and bad and ugly onto its pages and waits for you to react – good or bad.

I finally posted about my loss. So many shared their own sadness and miscarriages and I realised that social media was a great tool to bring together those who had lost babies. In those moments of weakness and pain and grief, I declared it all across social media so that everyone would hear about my baby. It brought so much comfort to those who had lost a baby themselves and in the subsequent years, and sadly my subsequent three losses, I had so many friends and old school acquaintances, like only social media can bind, contact me for advice for themselves or their relative or their friend who had just lost their baby. I could bring comfort and support and help, whilst also having a cathartic outlet for my own grief. But in the midst of the raw pain of my losses, each time I saw a Facebook announcement showing a grainy black-and-white scan image it caused me distress and anguish and the heartache of 'that should be me!' Social media and loss is a two-edged sword. It can offer great support but also unpredictable triggers. Someone's 'joke' pregnancy announcement or an announcement when you have just lost. Whatever it is, it is up to you the individual to decide whether it is a help or a hindrance that day, that hour, that minute, and to respond accordingly.

A few years on, I can see the great benefit social media brought for me. I feel that my vulnerability in sharing my losses has helped shape me. It is also where I first had contact with the Saying Goodbye charity, who then walked with me through three more losses and most importantly became my friends. For that I am truly grateful.

Sarah's Story

Baby loss can be a lonely place. It can be, but that wasn't my experience. As a self-confessed extrovert, I process the highs and lows in my life by discussing them with friends. Hairdressers. Taxi drivers. Total strangers. The day we lost our baby, while on a year travelling around the world, I decided to share our utter heartbreak on Instagram. I was sharing a daily travel caption anyway, and it felt right to share about this too.

I didn't want to treat miscarriage as a dirty secret, a taboo. I poured my heart out to my online friends, sharing the pain that I was feeling and acknowledging that I must not be alone. Chances were some people reading it would have experienced the same pain. What I didn't expect were the 700 messages and comments I received.

All of them supportive, and most of them – sadly – with a personal understanding of baby loss. Social media can get a bad rap but, in the most painful period of our lives, my husband and I found it nothing but a buoyancy aid. We clung to each other: talking till our voices were hoarse, dancing in the garden to music only we could hear, and crying hot, bitter tears. Then, when we needed to look outside of ourselves, we read messages from strangers.

They were so comforting. There is something beautifully infectious about honesty. I had messages from women who'd suffered a miscarriage but never told a soul other than their partner. I had messages from women who'd suffered numerous miscarriages and had emerged the other side, stronger.

But the best thing social media brought me was Zoë Clark-Coates. Zoë, in her selflessness, her kindness, supported me through the first days – and weeks – of losing my baby with practical advice alongside words of wisdom. I'd never met her at that point, but a friend had told me to send a message on Facebook. Zoë replied and immediately stepped into the role of mentor, guiding me through the entire experience. I'll never be able to thank her enough.

Special and Notable Occasions

Until you have lived a full year following the loss of your loved one, you have no idea what may become a key trigger (and even after that 12-month milestone new triggers can appear). There are, of course, key occasions to be aware of which may (and probably will) cause new grief layers to be pulled back. These are:

* Birthdays
* Anniversaries
* Due dates
* Mother's and Father's Day
* Baby Loss Awareness Month/Week
* Christmas and other widely celebrated holidays and occasions

I call the moments of grief that hit us from nowhere and bring us to our knees 'grief thunderbolts', and if we try to predict and pre-empt what may or may not cause them, we can become constantly fearful of the future. The bottom line is it is impossible to envisage when they might strike. Even unrelated deaths, events or occasions can trigger waves of baby-loss grief, as anything that taps into similar emotions can initiate a fresh wave to hit. We just have to bravely move forwards and deal with our reaction whenever and wherever these thunderbolts do strike us down.

Facing our grief is daring and it's bold; it takes real courage – looking loss directly in the eye and still choosing to steadily move towards it. We have to face these key occasions, whether we feel ready or not. What I can say to you to hopefully bring you some reassurance is this: 90 per cent of the time the fear of the event is much worse than the reality of actually walking through the occasion, so try going into events and key dates with an open mind and without preconceptions of how you 'may' feel. Just say to yourself, whatever I feel is okay. If I cry – that is okay. If another grief layer is harshly pulled off – that is fine. If I feel absolutely nothing – that is equally fine.

Some people choose to mark occasions by doing something special; others prefer to carry on as normal. I encourage you to do whatever you feel is right for you and your family. Remember this is your journey, your story – you write the rule book.

If you are looking for ideas, here are a few things that I know can help:

* Light a candle on special days
* Hang a Christmas decoration on the tree each year with your baby's name on it (this may be a nickname or simply say 'baby', with a date on it)
* Plant a tree or plant
* Donate money or time to a charity or cause in honour of your baby
* Carry out random acts of kindness in honour of your lost baby

* Visit a special place
* Read a special book which makes you feel connected to your baby

Baby-loss awareness

Baby Loss Awareness Day, Week and Month was first started back in 1988 by Ronald Reagan. In recent years it has become bigger and bigger, and now during the month of October the press and media are filled with stories that aim to start the conversation around baby loss. For some, this month encourages them to share their own stories and makes them feel less alone. For others, it can be really painful, as when you are in the depths of grief, or if you are suffering with any PTSD, seeing so many stories of loss can be a key trigger. For those who do want to embrace these events, I would encourage you to share your stories and posts on social media, and also just start the conversation among friends – because talking as a group can provide real healing to people who have locked their pain away.

This is something I wrote to thank people for sharing my posts and the charity's posts:

Baby Loss Awareness Message

I want to say something . . . I want to share from the heart . . .

Baby loss awareness is *not* for parents who have gone through loss – let me explain what I mean by that. Bereaved parents don't need a special day or week to remember; they remember their child 365 days a year, whether the world acknowledges their loss or not.

Whether their baby has been lost early or late in pregnancy, at birth or in early years, they remember.

Baby loss awareness is about shining a light on this subject, a subject that so many are afraid of and so many run from.

But I want to say this: baby loss is not just a story of grief, of pain and of tears; it is a story of love, of celebration, of becoming parents. It's a place where grief and love collide, it's where dreams lie shattered on the floor, but simultaneously where a new view of life can be birthed. It is only when the silent scream has been released from your soul when your heart has been broken in two that you discover this depth of love and pain even exists. So when the tears are falling, smiles are also breaking forth.

Baby loss is a journey, a lifelong journey, and if you have helped spread awareness let me say thank you. Thank you from me, but also thank you from every parent around the globe who has lost a child. Because when you shared their post, when you hit 'like', they saw you, they heard you. You showed them they were not the only one remembering their child; you were remembering them too.

So today and every day millions of us will celebrate our lives, we will find joy in the smallest of things, as this is the gift our lost children gave us. The space they left behind will always remain, for these are our children, and they made us parents.

Zoë x

Here is something you may like to read which relates to loss at Christmas. I wrote it a few years ago and it went viral on social media, which means it resonated with many, so it may help you.

What is Christmas like for those who have lost?

Well, we all know the true reason for Christmas and what we are celebrating.

A baby.

The baby.

That little miracle, who we know to be called Jesus.

Children have always been the centre of Christmas and, when you are longing for a child, Christmas can be one of the most heart-breaking times of the year.

Imagine this . . .

A nine-month walk of hope and longing.

At the end of the journey an empty crib.

No family and friends bringing gifts of joy and hope; often, in fact, no visitors, as most feel it too painful to set foot into this new world of devastation and mourning. Some worry they will not know what to say, others are so scared that this sort of tragedy could befall them that they choose to pretend this sort of loss doesn't exist. To do that means they need to avoid all baby loss, so they vanish from your world.

Some people who have lost a baby have been blessed to have other children, or perhaps had children before they lost their baby, so for those people the holidays are a mixture of joy and sadness. They have little ones to celebrate with, but they are acutely aware that they should be hanging more stockings on the fireplace, and that a crucial and wanted person is missing.

So as people all around the world put out mince pies for Santa, wrap presents, and excitedly anticipate the looks on their little ones' faces on Christmas morning, please take a moment to think of those who are still holding on for their miracle, and are missing . . .

A child they love.

A child they long to hold.

A child they would give the world to raise.

Occasions and events can encourage us to be more vulnerable, as we are often forced or persuaded to share our pain and stories with those around us. This in turn helps those who care for us, as they can better understand the pain that is being carried by their loved one (it also often gives them permission to share any pain and grief they may be personally carrying).

One of my favourite C. S. Lewis quotes is from his book *The Four Loves* (he wrote so eloquently about grief):

To love at all is to be vulnerable. Love anything and your heart will be wrung and possibly broken. If you want to make sure of keeping it intact you must give it to no one, not even an animal. Wrap it carefully round with hobbies and little luxuries; avoid all entanglements. Lock it up safe in the casket or coffin of your selfishness. But in that casket, safe, dark, motionless, airless, it will change. It will not be broken; it will become unbreakable, impenetrable, irredeemable. To love is to be vulnerable.

So let me encourage you to choose courage. To bravely reject society's often subtle message to deny one's grief and pain, in a bid to not disturb a happy equilibrium. Be vulnerable, however hard that may seem, as the more open you are, the more you will feel connected to those around you.

4

Post-Loss

TRYING FOR A CHILD POST-LOSS

This is such a big decision for some and a foregone conclusion for others. Perhaps it is best to start with my personal experience. Following the loss of our first baby, we very much dealt with that loss by just carrying on and not even talking about the miscarriage. In hindsight, that wasn't really dealing with the loss at all; it was simply surviving it. But it worked for us initially and, because of the way we processed the experience, we automatically started to try again for another baby, without much discussion.

After a relatively short period of time we found out we were pregnant again. This time felt different. We felt very positive that this time we would end up with a baby in our arms. Our first scan was magical and I can't even explain the joy we felt in seeing our little one on the screen, and the sound of the heartbeat that filled the room was truly beautiful.

I then started to bleed and we feared the worst, but a scan reassured us that all was well and our baby was fine. Shortly after, the bleeding recommenced and I felt sure that our baby had died. I am kind of reluctant to say it was mother's instinct, as I now know that when fear really takes a grip, it can lead you to assume your baby has died and often this hunch is proved wrong, but during that time I was convinced our daughter had died, and tragically this was confirmed a few days later. The bottom then firmly and dramatically fell from our world. Time stood still.

We chose to deliver her naturally and not have surgery, and without much information at our disposal we felt we were crawling around in the dark. A week to the day later, I went into labour and delivered her. This was one of the most painful nights of my life emotionally. Was it beautiful? Sadly, I can't say it was; I wish I could. I felt that while I was delivering my child, my heart was shattering into even more pieces. I screamed and sobbed on my bathroom floor for days, weeks, probably months.

Just like after our first loss we didn't feel we had a choice about whether to continue to try for another baby. My maternal instinct had kicked in so strongly, the thought of not having a child to raise was another source of grief I didn't feel able even to contemplate, so we just had to keep trying. Did we fear another loss? Of course we did, but the pain of not having any more children was greater than the fear.

Did we feel able and ready to handle another loss? No, but I don't think anyone would ever be ready to have their world shattered, so while we feared more loss, we knew we would need to just risk it all and try for another baby. So we tried again. We were scared. I was as scared of finding out I was pregnant as I was of finding out I wasn't pregnant each month.

Doing those pregnancy tests was both exciting and terrifying. My heart would race, I would feel sick and the panic was overwhelming. Whenever a test showed 'not pregnant' it felt like another wave of grief hit. A negative test meant we were back to square one and I would reopen my diary and work out all my fertile days for the next month. It felt like we were on a running machine going nowhere, but we could see an end destination where we had to be. The grief and loss cycle felt monotonous and never-ending.

I loved trying for a baby and that never changed, and I am truly grateful for that. For us it never felt routine or mandatory. It always felt romantic, passionate and beautiful.

I researched all the tips on how to maximise the chances of getting pregnant, and of course the top tips included things like having a pillow under your hips, putting your legs up a wall for 30 minutes post-sex, not showering for an hour or so after sex. Do they help? Who knows, but it is nice to feel you can do something to help the chances of conceiving, so we embraced them all.

Then we got that positive pregnancy test.

Fear – terror – elation – joy.

We then lost our third baby.

Shock – devastation – disbelief.

We immediately started to try again for another baby. I think a little denial clicked back in, to be honest, as I couldn't even begin to process what this all might mean for us. Did this mean we weren't able to carry a baby to term? Did it mean there was a major physical issue with myself or Andy? There were so many questions whizzing around my brain and I was too scared to address any of them.

Our dog of eleven years then died.

I didn't believe we could be any more shattered by this point, but losing our dog having lost our three precious children really did break us even more. I was utterly devastated. I was desperate to die. I wasn't suicidal, as I wouldn't ever have taken my own life – I would not have done that to Andy or my family – but I would have loved for something to have fallen from the sky and wiped me from the planet. The grief was intense, black and all-consuming. I couldn't eat, drink and was hardly able to function.

Having a third loss definitely made us think we might never have a child to raise and I could not see any hope on the horizon. I remember I kept saying to Andy, 'We can't do this again, we can't ever try again.' And he just kept saying that whatever I wanted was what he wanted. It felt like I was in the deepest of battles emotionally.

Then I realised my period was late. I did a pregnancy test in secret. I was pregnant – I cried with delight. I cried in fear. I cried with relief. This time it was different – we ended up with our little girl in our arms. Esme Emilia Promise, the daughter we had waited so very long for. When she was around two years of age, we decided we wanted her to have a sibling. We naively thought loss was behind us and started to try for a baby.

We were blessed to conceive fairly quickly and it was so exciting. Just like with our second pregnancy, we had been for regular scans and all was going well. Then on one tragic day at a routine scan appointment my consultant turned to me and said, 'Zoë, I am so sorry, your baby's heart has stopped beating.' Just like that; in the blink of an eye our world once again changed.

We chose to have surgery for the first time, mainly

because I didn't want to prolong it for Esme's sake. The operation went fine. Recovery post-op was fine. Emotionally I was back to being broken, but I was really good at hiding it from our daughter.

I was shocked how I was not only grieving the loss of our child (who we named Samuel), but I was also grieving the loss for Esme, who had also lost a brother. I was constantly thinking whether he would have looked like his sister. Would he have had the same infectious giggle and love of life? Would he have looked like his dad? Would he have had curly hair like Andy or straight like me? So many questions, all unanswered.

Trying again after losing Samuel was a bigger decision for us than previously. We were very aware that it wasn't just us needing to recover from loss – Esme was also now part of the equation. We were so desperate for another baby, however, and Esme kept asking for another brother or sister, so we decided to try again.

We were blessed to conceive and hoped and prayed this time would be different. Shortly after telling the family we were expecting, I began to bleed. A doctor told us we had miscarried again, and the shock was overwhelming. Something wasn't right, however. I kept getting sicker and sicker and eventually we booked in for a private scan. The scan showed I was still pregnant and the doctor had been wrong. A second scan then conformed we were in fact having twins. We then discovered a new type of shock!

Sadly, we went on to lose one of the twins. We named her Isabella. Bronte was then born at full term by emergency C-section.

So many people ask us whether we want more children,

and I can confirm that we decided to stop at two in our arms and five in heaven. Our family is now complete. As you can see, I speak from personal experience, and trying again post-loss is truly hard. The emotions you have to experience and process are huge and life-changing.

My top tips:

* Speak with your GP or medical team and ask them for advice and tips. Some useful questions to ask are: Could I be put on any drugs that might help? What vitamins should I be taking? Could they offer any tests to rule out issues – e.g. blood tests or scans? Am I physically ready to carry a baby?
* Try not to overthink the process of trying for a baby. There are so many tips on how best to conceive and when to try during the month. While some of this advice is helpful, it can also become all-consuming. If sex starts to be only about baby-making, it can damage a relationship and can certainly affect the intimacy you and your partner have between you.
* Keep talking as a couple. The better you communicate, the easier everything will be.
* Give yourself time to recover emotionally if you feel you need it. We are always told to ensure we are physically ready, but it is just as important to feel mentally ready for another pregnancy, or even emotionally ready to try to get pregnant.
* I would always advise people not to wait until they feel ready to lose again. Who would ever feel ready to lose another baby? It is like asking someone to wait to feel

ready to be pushed off the edge of a cliff. When you enter a new pregnancy, you do so with the belief that all will be different this time, and you can only do this if you have faith things will be okay, and while some may feel this is naïve, I believe it's holding on to hope with two hands.

* If you are blessed to get pregnant, consider telling people as soon as possible. The more people who know about your pregnancy, the more support you will be offered from those around you.

Losing the Desire to Have a Child

Many people message me in a complete panic when they suddenly feel that their desire to have another child has vanished. They worry what this will mean for their relationship (especially if their partner is 100 per cent committed to having another child) or for their living children, if this means they won't now be able to give them a brother or sister.

My initial response is always the same. Do not panic. Deep grief and trauma can often remove the desire to have more children for a period of time, due to the fear of encountering more loss. It is as if the brain is safeguarding the person from more trauma. This feeling rarely lasts indefinitely, and is more likely to be a transient state that will pass after a period of mourning, so try not to worry or overthink things if you wake up one morning without the burning desire to repopulate. I had this feeling after we lost our third baby. I just could not imagine going through more loss, and decided we would be much better off not trying for more children. Andy was so wonderful with me, and just kept reassuring me that if that's what I wanted he was totally fine with it. This simple reassurance took away any pressure and, within a few weeks, my desire to have a baby returned.

However, for some people the feelings do remain, and this can often be a cause of discontent in relationships. I always then advise sitting down with a counsellor as soon as possible so that all feelings can be aired, discussed and processed, in the hope that both parties can get on to the same page emotionally.

Adoption

Deciding to adopt after loss (or before loss) is sometimes a hard decision, and sometimes a very simple one, but it is always a personal choice and only the couple can know if it is right for them. I speak with many people each week who have explored adopting a child and some consider it and then rule it out, while others wonder why they didn't embark on the path a lot sooner. I hope that reading the stories within this chapter helps you in some way.

The first story is Helen's, who lost 14 babies before she and her partner Adam chose to start their adoption story. Then we hear from Anya, who had been through loss, has two living children with her, and then decided to expand their family further by adopting a little boy.

Helen's Story

After our last loss we finally came to the realisation that we were not going to be able to have children naturally. It wasn't a hard decision in the end – I had had a ruptured ectopic pregnancy and had ended up in emergency surgery. It was too dangerous to try again, so stopping was the only option.

My infertility hit me like a brick in the face. The stark realisation was that I was never going to be a mum to living children unless we looked at alternative options, and in the very beginning we just couldn't even think about that. We were both too lost in our own individual grieving. For a year we drifted on through life but I just couldn't stop my inner voice. What started as a whisper turned into a shout; I just couldn't picture my life in front of me without a child in it. I didn't want to be childless. I wanted to do the things that our friends and family were doing. Not just the big things – the holidays and first days of school and Christmas. The set pieces. I wanted to do the small things – the walking the dog together, eating Sunday dinner, brushing teeth, doing homework. The million and one routine things that were being carried out in family homes up and down the country. The things that weren't happening in our home that were making me feel so empty.

Adoption had always been a positive experience in my own family. My own dad was adopted and it was something that we had always embraced. It was natural, I think then, that I started to believe this was something we should look at. What I wasn't prepared for was my husband's reaction. Although he believed in adoption, I was totally gobsmacked when he told me that he didn't think it was for him and that he wasn't sure he could love a non-biological child as he would a birth child. He said he was happy that it was just the two of us. I obviously wasn't. On top of the desire to be a mum, I was also overloaded with guilt. The fact that I couldn't hold on to our babies and make him a father was a massive issue for me. I'd told him countless times to leave me and to have children with a woman who could. He'd always told me not to be stupid, but the guilt just wouldn't shift.

We played around the adoption question for a couple of years. I became more and more convinced that we should try. He stuck to his line – he just wasn't sure he could do it. And finally things came to a head. I knew that my need to be a mum wasn't going to go away. And that I had to explore options. I was becoming resentful of my husband's position and knew that I had to do this for me. So I told him I was going to go to an adoption agency and have a conversation. He could come with me. Or he could choose not to. But I wouldn't force him. I was making a decision for me. He needed to make his own mind up.

We didn't speak for a week. Then he told me he had been in contact with some work friends who had adopted and had chatted with them. He was willing to go to the agency they used and ask some questions. But he wouldn't commit to anything other than that. This was the turning point for us. An agreement from him that he was open to a discussion. A commitment from me not to push him. And that started the next stage of our life that ended up with us adopting our daughter. And if you asked my husband now, he couldn't love her any more than he does – he just needed to face the fear to try for her.

Anya's Story

I will always tell people that all three of our children are miracles and have been hugely fought for to be here. The story of our first two children spans six years of heartache, and the many highs and lows of fertility treatment. Our daughter Hope was our first IVF cycle and we were given odds of 1 in 125,000 that we would ever conceive naturally. Our son Barnaby was born after three more failed cycles, two early pregnancy losses and years of tears and frustrations. He was our fifth cycle and would certainly have been our last. Against all the odds he, too, was conceived and our family of four finally felt at peace.

Yet there had always been a question mark for us over the role of adoption. Having been told early on that we would struggle to conceive, we began looking at adoption even when we were first investigating treatment. It always felt a positive and good thing to do, and the issue around genetics and nature/nurture for us was always to be held lightly and prayerfully.

The seed was planted, and we waited and prayed until Barney was about four before starting to really investigate this as an option.

Compared to the stresses of IVF, the actual process to

become adoptive parents really did feel much easier for us. Comparatively, months of filling in forms and social-worker meetings were far easier than injections and uncertainty. It was a lengthy process, with huge time commitments, but it all felt quite doable.

We felt encouraged by close friends who adopted at the same time and the overall feeling that adoption can be a positive and good thing to do.

As Christians, we also felt called to open our home and to welcome in a child, giving them a second chance at a life that they wouldn't otherwise have had. We realised we were far from perfect as a family but that we had the capacity to love and care for another child.

The whole process took around three years from start to finish and until we were finally matched with our son Christopher and brought him home to be his forever family. That was five years ago, and we are now a family of five and still learning every day.

I still maintain that adoption is an incredible thing and our son is ours completely, but I would be lying if I also didn't say it's been the hardest thing we have ever done. Adoption isn't just 'normal' parenting; it's parenting a child with a history of trauma and, in our case, with additional needs brought on by fetal alcohol spectrum disorder. We have had to relearn how to parent considering this and have had to adjust many of our expectations of what our new life would look like. It is sometimes exhausting, often complicated, and has pushed us as a family to our limits. But so often the most worthwhile things are also the costliest in this life and we can see the changes, even the smaller ones, that are occurring in our son, and it is incredible.

Adoption is very often focused on in terms of the

process and the pre-adoption matching. This is the case with professionals and often the people around us, family and friends. Yet adoption needs greater focus after a child is placed, and there is a huge lack of support and care set up for adopters to access easily.

The phrase 'it takes a village to raise a child' had never really meant that much to me before adopting Chris, but now we know just how true that is. We are needing the support of so many professionals, the adoption community as well as care from family or friends just to walk this path. Yet we remain hopeful that it is a path worth taking and one with enormous repercussions. Adoption is an amazing option; certainly not one for everyone, but an amazing one nevertheless. And our three children are testimony to the fight being worth it all.

Pregnancy Post-Loss

The most important thing I want you to know and remember is this:

> *No baby can or will ever replace another.*
> *Every single baby is unique and precious.*
> *Any child that is born following a baby*
> *that has died is not a replacement –*
> *they are a longed-for sibling and*
> *a gift to their family.*

I know I was personally so worried that people would think I was replacing the children I had lost, and this bothered me a lot, as it couldn't be further from the truth. It also worried me for another reason when people said things like this to me, and that reason was I didn't want my living children to feel like they were a replacement – as they have never been, and will never be, that.

People often ask me why parents are concerned about this, and I am quick to educate them that these feelings are often born as a result of people saying things like, 'Now you can move on' or, 'Now you have another baby to focus on.' While these comments often come from people with good hearts, who have just said the wrong thing in the moment, they fuel the fire of this fear and it can stop some from trying for more children, or make them reluctant to share news of subsequent pregnancies.

If you are worried about having more children for this reason, I ask you to soak up these words and let them become your inner voice: Any future children I am blessed to have will not replace the child that died; they will be a brother or sister to them, and that means more people to cherish the memories and talk of their existence.

Let's jump forwards and presume you have taken the steps needed to grow your family further and your heart is now racing, wondering if you should do a pregnancy test. You will probably be terrified of a negative pregnancy test, and terrified of a positive test. I have been there – I have weed on that stick (hundreds of sticks, if I am honest). I remember my heart pounding fit to burst out of my chest, and feeling sick at the thought of jumping back on to that pregnancy rollercoaster, which to me meant no peace of mind for nine months, but also the utter thrill of antici- pation that this could mean I get a longed-for baby in my arms.

Firstly, let us deal with the sad news when the pregnancy test is negative. This can be heart-breaking, and can even make the full weight of the grief hit you afresh. In that moment, you feel devastation and wonder if you will ever get the child you long for. Tears stream and dreams swiftly exit the bathroom window. I can't give you a miracle cure for this sadness; all I can say is let those tears fall. You are grieving for the baby(ies) you have lost, and also grieving for the lack of pregnancy you hoped for. This is normal. It usually takes people a few days or a few weeks to recompose themselves and focus on a fresh month of trying again. But know it is 100 per cent normal for each negative pregnancy test to reveal a new layer of grief.

Now let us look at when you get that positive test. If you initially feel scared or even terrified, please don't feel like a bad person. Fear in no way negates the joy and gratitude you feel to be pregnant, and after going through any loss, of course, you may be apprehensive and nervous about starting a pregnancy marathon yet again, especially when you may not even have regained the strength from a previous loss. The shock of seeing the two lines on the pregnancy test can take days or weeks to pass, so just allow yourself time to adjust to this new reality. Make sure that you are taking prenatal vitamins and visit your GP as quickly as possible to ensure your pregnancy can be medically recorded, as this means they can help you with the emotional support you may need.

I could fill a whole book with advice and support regarding pregnancy post-loss (and I am currently writing that one next), but here are some valuable pointers:

1. Tell people you are pregnant as soon as you feel ready. I am a big believer in breaking the 12-week rule of not telling anyone until after your first scan. To me this is a 'not so subtle' message to not share about loss. We need support when we have good or bad news, so tell your family, tell your friends – shout it from the rooftop that you are pregnant. Enjoy every single second from day one: you have created a child – it's a miracle of life and one that should be celebrated from the outset.

2. Be open with your doctors, midwives and other med-

ical professionals about your medical history. If they know what you have journeyed through they will be able to support you better.

3. If you don't get good compassionate care from your doctor, midwife, etc., ask to see a different one. No one needs to stay under the care of medical staff who don't support them fully or make them feel confident in their care. So don't fear offending people, just ask to transfer care.

4. If you live in a large area and have multiple choices for hospital care, you may want to consider being looked after by a different hospital. For some, changing hospitals/clinics/practices helps them cope emotionally.

5. Consider getting reassurance scans if you are worried. It is 100 per cent natural to be more concerned in pregnancies post-loss, and that means a person may need more appointments, scans or Doppler checks to gain peace of mind and that is okay.

6. Know it is normal to worry about all aches and pains. Most pregnant ladies who have sadly lost a baby in the past will tell you they become completely paranoid about every twinge and ache. They fret about having too many symptoms as well as if they lack symptoms. Please don't worry in silence – tell your GP or midwife and let them bring you much-needed reassurance.

7. Fear of using the loo in case you see blood is again totally normal. For more information on this, see 'Fear Post-Loss' on page 114.

8. Fear of doing normal everyday tasks and exercises in case you trigger a loss. Firstly, please know this is something the majority of women worry about in pregnancy post-loss, and the fear usually settles as the

pregnancy progresses. Again, talk to your GP and mid-wife as they should be able to reassure you about daily activities.

9. Talk to your partner, if you have one, or a friend or family member if not. The more you talk about any fears or worries you have, the easier it is to get through the nine months of pregnancy. Keeping things bottled up helps no one, and it can actually make the fear grow.

10. Don't try to prepare yourself for loss and postpone celebrating the pregnancy for fear that it may end in grief. You cannot prepare for baby loss; if the worst happens, you deal with it then, and by not embracing your pregnancy you are just robbing yourself of the joy you could be experiencing today. One of my favourite quotes is: 'worrying is like walking around with your umbrella up just in case it rains'. Oh, how true this is. Worry does not prevent pain, just like an umbrella doesn't stop the rain. We just miss out on happy moments, on enjoying those often-fleeting seconds where everything feels perfect. So, if you are blessed to find out you are carrying a baby, give yourself the gift and the freedom to embrace the joy; go all in and pray you make it to the finish line and bring a baby home in your arms. Because in that moment all is well; in that second you are having a healthy baby.

The Mariposa Trust asked 224 people about their experience of pregnancy having previously lost a baby. Here are the results:

* 96.77% of people said they were scared during subsequent pregnancies, with 81.57% saying the fear lasted throughout the pregnancy.

When asked how quickly they tried for another child:

* 48.65% started trying within three months of losing a baby
* 22.07% started trying within six months of losing a baby
* 10.81% started trying within 9–12 months of losing a baby
* 18.47% started trying 12+ months after losing a baby

Sarah's Story

I compare my experience of pregnancy after loss as similar to being on a fairground ride.

Throughout the nine months I experienced highs and lows; there were obvious milestones I wanted to get to – my reassurance scan, 12-week scan, 20-week scan. I would tell myself that, once reached, my anxiety would disappear, I could relax and enjoy the experience, but the truth is that the peaks of anxiety kept coming. Although, with hindsight, I can see that I was able to enjoy myself too.

I previously experienced a missed miscarriage and so my fear in this pregnancy was loss of my baby's heartbeat. I avoided announcing my pregnancy to my wider circle of friends for as long as possible in an attempt to protect myself from the pain of another loss.

As soon as you become pregnant, you open yourself up to the possibility of hurt, but you also open yourself up to loving another person unconditionally. I had an overwhelming feeling of anger and sadness – the innocence and initial excitement I felt I should have had with pregnancy had been taken away from me. I was all too aware of complications.

I combated my fears by talking honestly with my

midwife. At each appointment, the first check she undertook was for the heartbeat and I had an appointment every two weeks. It was good to be heard and understood.

Having experienced loss, I feel I treasured this pregnancy that little bit more than I had the first time. At the time, the nine months felt endless. Looking back now, it was over in a heartbeat and I finally had my baby in my arms. Ultimately, I had to trust in my body and believe that my baby would do everything he could to be with me. My mantra was: 'this baby wants to be born'.

Emily's Story

When I saw the second line on the pregnancy stick, I did not feel joy and excitement, I felt fear and dread. When I told my husband, his response was, 'Okay, well, here we go again,' and I couldn't have agreed with his comment more, that just about summed it up. After experiencing miscarriage, I found being pregnant after loss terrifying. I felt all-consumed with fear, and then angry that my miscarriages had robbed me of the joy of pregnancy.

Throughout my pregnancy sickness, people often said, 'It'll all be worth it.' I just thought, 'Well, it wasn't the previous times.' I was terrified of going to the loo in case I saw red, terrified of every twinge, every ache or even of feeling less sick! I presumed I would be fine after the 12-week scan, but I wasn't, the fear was just as intense. Now people would talk about my baby's arrival as a sure thing, but to me, I had 100 per cent success rate in my babies dying – what proof did they have that this one would be different? I had pregnancy insomnia from week 17 due to anxiety about the pregnancy. I was constantly checking and mentally recording the baby's movements, which is exhausting and put me in a constant state of worry and tension. I was frequently in the maternity ward being monitored, panicking that something had gone wrong.

I did give birth to a beautiful, healthy little girl we've named Alyvia. I fully and wholeheartedly grasp how lucky and blessed we are. However, it did take both my husband and I four months before we truly believed that we would get to keep her and watch her grow up. The new fear of cot death or other complications was sometimes all-consuming – we once visited A&E only to be told she was 'a perfect picture of health'. We have both been prescribed anti-anxiety medication from the GP and have had to practise meditation, exercise and take part in counselling to manage our anxiety. I don't think you can overestimate the huge impact loss can have on subsequent pregnancies and on your mental health.

Not Being Able to Have Another Child

Whether it be by choice, circumstance or due to medical reasons, not being able to have another child post-loss can be exceptionally hard to accept and process, and it can feel like another bereavement in itself. It is not at all simple to relinquish the desire to grow a family, and anyone who makes it seem easy is doing a huge disservice to those who are going through this hell.

For some, not having more children may mean they never have a child to raise at all, and for others it means having a much smaller family than the one they desired to have. Either way, this loss needs to be expressed, acknowledged and processed.

Janey's Story

We had our son following loss and I loved him, instantly. I know that the 'bonding' process varies but I'm being completely honest when I say it was there for me the moment I saw him. He was perfect and I was overwhelmed by how much love I had for someone I had only just met and how much my life changed in that flicker of time. No one could ever tell me quite how wonderful it was going to be.

I would've loved to experience that all again but was so scared to try again, and we had such contentment within our family.

Eventually we did try, and it saddened me so much, after three more losses, that we decided to count our blessings and live for the now.

I thought that sadness would always be my own. However, the hardest part of that decision comes now – my son desperately wants a baby sibling; every dandelion wish for one hurts so deeply. He is too young to understand, and I would never want to burden him with something so sad. All I can give him is unconditional love. The support and encouragement he will ever need to be the person he wants to become. The knowledge that he will always be a part of a loving and caring family, and he will always have a safe place to call home.

Amie's Story

My husband and I got married in December 2008 when I was 36, so we decided to try for a baby right away. In August 2009 I fell pregnant but a few weeks later I had a miscarriage. Luckily, I got pregnant in January 2010 and had our daughter in October that year. We waited a few years as we were just enjoying her but, given my age, we felt it was time to start trying again. We tried for quite some time, and nothing happened. I then got all the NHS checks and they came back normal, so we decided on IVF in early 2015. I did get pregnant but also had a miscarriage.

Along this journey, I only really had my husband and a few friends for support, no real advice or help was given at the hospital. The miscarriages, all the tests and IVF were so invasive; my body didn't feel like it was mine any more. Following the IVF miscarriage, we decided to relax and think about whether we would keep trying or stop. Later in 2015 we tried again and, by miracle, I found out I was pregnant on Boxing Day. There were many mixed emotions but, because of all the heartache in the past, we just didn't feel excited.

I felt numb and worried up to my 13-week scan, where we unfortunately found out that something was wrong with the baby. Ultimately, we had to make the horrific and devastating decision to end the pregnancy; along with that came several invasive procedures and a funeral.

By this stage of the process (trying for a second child) I had one living child and three babies in heaven. So, you see, Lois isn't an only child but she's my only child on earth who I'm able to cuddle, love and devote my time to. Enough, right? That's the question I asked myself after longing for another child. A child to grow up with a big sister and complete our family. Why? We felt that two was perfect – I mean, who wants to grow up an only child? I think there is an assumption that having a second child will be easy – it happened once, it'll happen again. When it doesn't, it is a disappointment. I also felt very guilty for feeling this way. I have a healthy, lovely daughter but the longing for a second child wouldn't go away. Why is my one, who I love deeply, not enough? Who is she going to play with? Who will she tell her secrets to? Who will she moan about us to? We had this and so should she.

The longing didn't go away. I wanted to feel a pregnant belly, the kicks, the hiccups. I wanted to feel the smoothness of baby skin, kiss my newborn's head again, hear the first cry, watch the first steps, first word and first day of school, only this time with the confidence of experience.

It's still tough seeing pregnant women and babies, or talk of what is to be expected. It's painful when people say, 'Oh, just the one then', especially when you feel guilty for thinking this too.

I had therapy and it was reassuring to talk to someone who was unbiased and just listened with no judgement. She put it into perspective by affirming that the longing for what I perceived as the perfect family was a long journey when it painfully came to an end. That's eight years of trying, yearning and heartache. I still have moments of desire but mostly I embrace and cherish what I have. The therapist helped me to appreciate what I have but also to see that it's okay to feel sadness, without guilt. Learning how to balance the two has made me a better person.

Katy's Story

The flip of my stomach and the sting of tears behind my eyes is a feeling that I recognise all too well. This time it was Instagram. A gorgeous photo of a lady in a long, fitted dress, her huge bump proudly on show and the title 'Three weeks to go!' She looked beautiful and, even though she's a grown woman, I still saw the child in her that I used to teach. A quiet seven-year-old, attentive, always looking up to me and wanting to be just like me. 'So exciting! Sending love xxx', I wrote. I was happy for her but waves of grief cut my eyes and heavied my heart.

Four pregnancies, four miracles, four deaths. Every day while I work and carry on life's chores, I do the maths. 'Today is a third birthday! She'd be four now. He'd be six today! Just imagine a birthday party for a six-year-old! What cake would I buy? Or would I make it? What if they'd all lived? There would be beautiful chaos at that party.' There's new maths that I do every day now too. 'If I could sell my house by next year, maybe I could support myself and start IVF, then could I be pregnant again by next Christmas? I'd be 33. I'd be 34. I'd be 35.' Now, as the hope dims, 'I'd be 37.' Hope feels like a dangerous thing. It taunts me, reminds me that there's a chance but that time is running out. I'm on my own but is it possible? Is there a chance?

I distract myself and flick through Facebook but before my eyes register what I've seen my stomach flips. 'We're having a boy!' They have one of each now. Do they understand? Do they know how lucky they are? What must it feel like, that confident association between a positive test and a living baby? I can't imagine it.

Life keeps moving, work gets done, the shopping gets put in the trolley, but not all of me is there. A piece of me left when my babies died. As the years pass, I keep learning. I have grown, I am strong. I've learnt more about myself, empathy, grief and how to really give more support than most people do in a lifetime. Tragedy teaches you, the healing teaches you. They leave you new gifts but I'd hand all of that back in a heartbeat for just a moment of holding my babies in my arms.

Andrew's Story

(A FATHER'S EXPERIENCE)

When I met Catharine we were soon talking about marriage, starting a family. Our daughter, Grace, was conceived naturally and was carried to term before she died in the early stages of labour in April 2011. She was my first, and will be my only child.

Medical complications during the birth resulted in an extreme loss of blood, my wife's collapse and a three-hour operation to try to save my wife's life. I was left literally holding the baby and, in those dark hours, it crossed my mind more than once that I would walk out of the hospital alone.

It's hard to stay strong and carry on when all you want to do is cry. Being a man, carry on is exactly what I tried to do. Badly.

One October morning while walking to the train station for my 30-mile commute, I saw a rainbow, and on seeing the colours I lost it and broke down. I didn't get into the office that day, or for the next three months. The GP diagnosed PTSD.

The counsellor to whom I was referred quickly realised I had bottled everything up and I needed to tell my story – from A to Z, and if I missed anything I'd go back, slot the memory in and continue from there. We met three times a week and it took a month, and countless tissues, for me to finish the story. A weight lifted.

The next challenge was to try to change the image in my mind when I thought of the situation I found myself in. Working through the photographs, one was selected. A photograph that would in time bring happier thoughts, not pain.

The counsellor also suggested I should write. Having written poetry beforehand, this was the medium selected. After a number of aborted verses, time and more tissues, a poem, 'The Rainbow', was drafted, taking me back to that October day and putting a different perspective in my memory.

Story told, picture selected and poem written, the grief eased. I could see a way forward. We would try to conceive again.

The medical complications during Grace's delivery meant we had to ride the rollercoaster of IVF. Life created twice but no happy ending.

This setback put us both back in counselling. We could have carried on but many conversations later we decided to stop, a gradual realisation that we would have no living children. We also concluded that neither adoption nor fostering was for us. We would focus on us, on the love between us which grows deeper. We found our own ways to remember and honour Grace. Our mantra was, and still is, the two of us together with Grace in our hearts is enough.

I'll never again hold my child in my arms, but she is in my heart. Sometimes I struggle with having no living chil-dren, but then I look at that chosen photo of Grace, now the wallpaper on my phone. Or a timely rainbow appears in the sky and draws me back to those words penned in the autumn of 2011. Both make me smile.

Grief is a journey, and different for everyone. Through counselling I found me again. I needed to let the emotion out. Not bottle it up. By doing that I survived.

This isn't a road I would have chosen. The journey has changed me, but looking at me now, I like the man I have become. Yes, I would want Grace to have lived, but she is with me, carried in my heart and is only a word away.

Supporting the Bereaved

There are so many ways we can all help the bereaved, and what I would love this book to do is empower you to reach out with confidence to someone who has lost a baby. The fact that you are even trying to educate yourself on this subject and are researching how best to support someone means *you* are the right person for the job. You want to be the best support you can be, and that makes you one amazing person, so I want to thank you for taking the time to learn about this complex subject.

When I went through loss, I so appreciated those who offered me a hand of support. Some people took to supporting me like a duck to water; others were visibly treading water and were trying to look like they could swim. I appreciated each and every one of them. Those who said amazing things, those who stumbled over their words, and even those who said things that really shouldn't have been said. I loved that they tried; I appreciated that they cared enough to sit with me, even if they didn't feel comfortable doing so. So please don't be worried; just be there whenever they need you, love them, sprinkle kindness on them and be willing to step outside of your comfort zone.

Now, I'm going to warn you that some of my suggestions

may seem quite direct. I never want people to feel told off, or judged, or panicked, but I do want you to feel fully informed. I want to equip you with the right empathy tools, and the best way to do that is to tell you some commonly said things that can cause offence, and also some good things to say that can bring comfort. It would be easy for me to tiptoe around this, but that won't help you, or help the people you want to support, so I am going to be direct and say it how it is in the hope you can receive it in love.

If you read something in the 'do not say this' section and you have said it, please don't panic. I don't want anyone to feel shame or guilt. All of us can and will have said the wrong things, me included (probably many times a day!), so don't beat yourself up. Instead, say, 'Okay, I will know what to say next time.' If you feel you may have caused unintentional pain to someone in the past, you may, of course, want to address that, and I would purely suggest saying something along the lines of this: 'Having read *The Baby Loss Guide* I have learnt I may have said some insensitive things in the past. I trust you know my heart has only ever been to help you, but if I ever caused you additional pain, I am so sorry. I now feel better equipped to support you and others, and please always feel free to tell me if I say anything wrong in the future.' Saying something as simple as this is the ultimate olive branch, and can bring so much healing to unhealed wounds.

My Best Advice

Don't compare

Every journey is unique; therefore, even if you have been through something similar it will be different from the person in front of you, so don't rush to share your story about grief or loss, or say, 'This is how I felt, do you?'

Let them tell you their story first in their own words. By doing this the attention will also be kept on the person who's hurting, rather than transferring to you. If you have lost two babies and they have lost two babies, your stories may have significant similarities, but your journey through grief will be surprisingly different. Once they have shared, then open up about your story if you feel able.

One of my most precious times when I was at the rawest point of grief was when a friend sat on my bed and shared her experience of loss; it did make me feel less alone, so choose your words carefully and pick your moment wisely.

Be present

When researching this book, I asked people about the things said to them that caused pain. Perhaps not surprisingly, I received a long list, but one of the things that most people agreed on was that being there, and showing up, even if at times the wrong things were said, mattered more to them.

Having people avoid you, or avoid the topic of loss, causes way more pain than stumbling with words, or being a tad insensitive. So be brave and show up, however uncomfortable it makes you feel. Remember, you don't need to say anything; just hold the tissues, tell them you care and want to listen.

Accept you can't fix it

Part of showing up and being present for the grieving is having to accept that you can't fix it for the person.

Everything within you will want to make it better for them, as human instinct is to try to relieve another's suffering, but that's not possible when it comes to grief.

If you see it as your job to fix it, or to remove it, then, of course, very quickly you will feel overwhelmed in your task of offering support, as it is an impossible job and the goal will never be achieved. You will then begin to feel helpless and may start to panic; you may even want to run for cover as it could feel too hard to be that shoulder to cry on.

To avoid this happening, be aware that you will have an urge to fix it, but choose to accept that you can't. This acceptance will give you the freedom to just be you; you will realise that all you have the power to do is to listen, to offer support without judgement and without providing temporary fixes, and I promise you this will be a gift to the person who is grieving.

Never minimise

When we are supporting the bereaved, we need to be careful never to minimise their grief, or oversimplify the walk through loss. I would recommend not to start a sentence with 'at least', as 99 per cent of the time that will be a form of minimising a person's pain – for example, 'At least they aren't in pain', 'At least you can get pregnant', 'At least you aren't infertile', etc.

There is *no* 'at least' in grief support.

Be aware of what they have lost

It is easy to forget that when people lose a baby, they aren't just missing a newborn. They are also losing their toddler taking their first step. Their infant starting to read. Their teenager graduating from high school. Their grown child getting married to the love of their life. They are losing every magical moment. In the blink of an eye, the future has been erased.

Remembering this transforms how we offer support to bereaved parents, as you become aware of why the journey through grief does take a lifetime. The person will be mourning another stage of loss, another moment stolen from them, until the day they die.

Frequently Asked Questions

Can you move on following loss?

I often witness people talking about those who are grieving. Some of the most common comments appear to be: 'They seem to be stuck in grief' or 'They just haven't been able to move on'. These statements are used whenever a period of time has passed since the death of the loved one and the person is still talking about the loss, or showing visible signs of grief.

Firstly, grief and loss are not something one 'gets over', so just because someone is talking about the loss still, or is displaying symptoms of grief, this in no way means they are 'stuck'; it merely means they are processing, and that could be something they do for the rest of their life.

The loss of a loved one becomes part of who you are, and you learn to carry the weight of the grief and allow it to shape you into a different person.

How can we help people get to this stage in their grief journey?

By allowing them space to talk and share. If we try to rush people to process pain, it has the reverse effect and sets them back in their walk, so all we can do is walk alongside them and hopefully you will then start to witness them rediscovering their joy.

Can you become stuck in grief?

People often come to me saying their family member or friend is stuck in grief, and how can we help them as a charity.

My first question is what do you mean by 'stuck'? Just because someone is talking about their lost baby, it does not mean they are stuck. Just because someone is still weeping and heartbroken, it does not mean they are stuck. That is how grief works; they are meant to still talk about their loss, and they are grieving healthily if they still communicate about the one they have lost.

My worry is for the person who can't talk about their pain, and for the one who makes it seem like no loss has even happened.

So, is it possible to get stuck in grief? Yes, I believe it is.

I would question (and notice I say question, not assume) whether someone was stuck if their loss was a long time ago but they were still finding it impossible to talk about anything other than their pain. I would also consider whether someone was stuck if (after a substantial amount of time) they felt it impossible to move forwards in ordinary life because of being consumed by sorrow.

However, that said, there are no set rules and no set

formulas when it comes to moving through the grieving process. One plus one doesn't always equal two when it comes to grief.

What can we do if we think someone is stuck?

There is only one thing anyone can do and that is listen to their story. Hear their pain. Validate their experience. Show you care. People mostly get stuck because they are feeling a need to defend their right to be experiencing pain, as they don't feel their story is being heard. They may also feel the need to ensure their loved one is being acknowledged and not forgotten (this is especially true for baby loss). Simply by listening, we can help them unstick themselves.

Can you get closure?

Closure following a loss is as much of a myth as unicorns and fairy tales. One cannot close the door on grief. It is just not possible to put all feelings into a box, seal the lid and consider it part of the past. One can only learn to accept what has happened and learn to live with this new state of reality.

Does publicly grieving help?

Public grieving helps because we can suddenly see we are not alone in our pain. There is a reason we hold funerals, there is a reason that people around the world gather to celebrate the lives of those who have died, and that reason is that something powerful happens when we stand together. We feel supported. We feel less alone. We feel our loved one has been duly honoured. We feel our pain and loss have been recognised. Seeing all of this and exploring all of this helps hearts begin to mend.

One of the most vital things the Mariposa Trust does is run the international Saying Goodbye services. These public events are held at cathedrals, and they allow people from every generation a time and place to publicly grieve and acknowledge every baby they or someone else has lost. The services aren't about 'closure', they aren't an opportunity for people to formally say goodbye so they can 'move on', but are about healing the pain, acknowledging a baby existed, honouring the love that did and will always exist and giving space for people to say publicly, 'My baby matters.'

How do you know if someone is depressed or grieving?

You won't know this, and often the bereaved person may not even know it. I will always look for signs of depression in a person if they have suffered from depression pre-loss. Grief tends to come in waves; depression doesn't move, it stays like a black cloud. Grief can trigger depression. Grief can develop into depression. However, mostly grief stays as grief and is not 'depression' at all.

Be careful with how you word questions about how they are feeling and encourage them to share their worries and concerns. GPs are trained to help people determine whether they are depressed, so I would always encourage a person to sit with a doctor and talk about their feelings and symptoms, and then the doctor can advise them on what is best to do next.

A big alarm bell for me would be talk or mention of

suicide. There is a *big* difference between someone not wanting to live (because of the depth of the pain they are experiencing and the overwhelming feelings of missing the person they have lost) and being suicidal.

It is very common not to want to be here any more – who would want to live in agony daily and see no chance of respite on the horizon? Being suicidal is very different and if someone is considering ending their life or you feel he or she is at risk of this, encourage them to seek urgent medical help.

Things Not to Say and Why

I am regularly asked by people and the media what people shouldn't say. I prefer to focus on the right things to say, but I can also see a real benefit in highlighting the pitfalls and the things that are habitually told to the bereaved. So here goes – buckle up, my friends, and let me take you on a journey of clichés and the reasons why they cause pain.

'Let go'

If you say to someone, 'Let go of the pain' or 'You need to let go of your loved one now and just move on', you will be causing deep hurt, and I know that is the last thing you would want to do.

It's not possible to 'let go' of someone you have loved and lost, emotion doesn't work like that. In fact, love doesn't work like that. Although someone is no longer living life with a person in the physical sense, the love for them is acutely present. The only thing they need you to do is walk with them, help them to carry the load any way you can, journey with them as they learn to juggle the mammoth task of processing grief and pain while remaining present in the world.

'Perhaps you can't carry girls/boys?'

This guessing doesn't help anyone, and even though you are trying to find a reason in your mind why someone may have lost a baby, so that it makes sense to you, it helps no one and brings more pain to the grieving parent.

'It is time to move on/get over it/stop talking about it!'

Grief is not something one gets over and talking about the pain of loss is the best way for people to start to heal, so this needs to be encouraged and never discouraged.

'Heaven needed another angel'/'God didn't want them to stay'/'They are in a better place now they are in heaven'

This is just so painful and insensitive. Avoid bringing God into the conversation, as whether a person has faith or not, God didn't make this happen and trying to insinuate that their baby is in a better place says their home is not the best place for a child, which is hurtful.

'Time will heal your pain'/'Life goes on'

Yes, at times pain can decrease over time; however, it can also increase. No bereaved parent will thank you for telling them that life will get better down the line, while they are in the depths of grief, so avoid telling them it will. Just let them focus on today, as that can seem daunting enough when you are journeying through loss.

'At least you can have children'/'At least you aren't infertile'

We already know this should never be said, because it starts with 'at least' (see page 203) but let's focus on the sentiment rather than the phrasing.

When people are told to be grateful that they can have children following loss it is insulting for two reasons. Firstly, it is insulting, as of course those who have been able to conceive are grateful for that – why wouldn't they be? Secondly, they are highly likely to be screaming in their head, 'Yes, I am grateful I can get pregnant, but that's not much use if I can't stay pregnant or have a baby to raise!' Gratitude for anything doesn't negate the pain of loss or remove the permission or ability to grieve. Likewise, looking on the bright side of something doesn't take away the pain of loss, so we should encourage the bereaved to face the pain, not go on a hunt for a positive angle.

'At least you are still young enough to try again'

Another 'at least' to be avoided. Just because someone is young and appears to have many more fertile years ahead of them doesn't mean they will grieve any less for the baby they have lost.

'Are you planning to have another one?'

By asking a bereaved parent to focus on having another baby, it can feel like you are removing their permission to grieve for the baby they have just lost. It can also suggest you believe having another baby will replace the one they have lost, which is wrong and hurtful. Additionally, many people will say that they can't ever face the thought of having another baby in the weeks and months that follow loss, and it is entirely normal to feel that way, but it doesn't mean they will feel that way in six months, or in two years' time. Initially, it's hard to even decide what to eat for breakfast, let alone trying to make significant life choices. If we can avoid asking the bereaved to focus on these big life questions while they are in the depths of grief that can be a real help.

'You are lucky you already have children'

Of course, every child is a real blessing, but having children doesn't remove the grief you feel for the child you have lost. Let us imagine a situation where you have two children, and I turn to you and say, 'Which of your children are you willing to lose? You can only keep one of them!' You would never be able to answer and neither should you, yet when a bereaved parent loses a baby, often people expect them to be grateful for the one (or more) they still have with them. It is bizarre and insulting.

'You are blessed you have your health'/'At least you have a husband/partner'

This is another 'let's search for a blessing' ideology, in the hope it will negate the pain. It doesn't work; let's not do it.

'This is super-common, you know'

Yes, it's common; however, that does not make it less painful, or something one should expect. Getting cancer is sadly common too, but no one would ever think to go up to someone recently diagnosed and tell them so, yet people do this often with parents who have lost a baby.

'Because you have been through it before, you can cope again'

Just because someone has survived one loss, it does not automatically make them better equipped to deal with it a second, third or fourth time. Yes, a loss may have taught them some valuable life lessons or coping skills, but this can never be presumed, and should certainly never be spoken out loud. Every loss is different, and personality, life circumstances, emotional stability, physical health, etc. all play a part in how people cope.

'What doesn't kill you makes you stronger'

Let's avoid this commonly voiced cliché.

'Just try again'

Oh, how simple this sounds, and if only it were that straightforward. I am sure you can see how hurtful this would be to someone, but so many people say it. Trying again, and being blessed to conceive again, does not remove the pain of losing a previous baby, so it should never be said in grief support.

'Once you have another baby your pain will go'

Entirely untrue, and no bereaved parent would ever agree. It should never be thought or communicated. Another baby will never replace a baby that has died, and while other children are an absolute gift and blessing, their presence doesn't take away the pain of loss for the child that has died.

'Your womb was just being prepared for another baby'

This was said to me so many times, and again it is untrue. A womb doesn't need preparation; if that were the case, four out of four babies would be lost through miscarriage, rather than one in four. It is an old wives' tale which is still sadly repeated a lot to people who encounter miscarriage.

'Most people lose their first baby'

Again, not correct. The majority don't lose a baby; only one in four pregnancies are lost through miscarriage, so trying to make it seem like this happens to everyone is yet another way of devaluing grief and the experience of baby loss.

'In other countries, people expect to lose a child; it's only here we don't'

This may be true, but showing someone how privileged we are to live in this country doesn't help their pain. You are just subtly (or possibly not so subtly) removing their permission to grieve.

'My friend lost a baby at term/via cot death – that is much worse, isn't it?'

Comparison helps no one. There is no score attributable to grief and loss. Why does one have to be worse than another? Instead, let's stand together and say all loss is horrid, every baby lost is traumatic, and every parent and person touched by loss deserves to and should be supported.

'Do you think it may be something you did that caused it?'

I hear this asked all the time, and it makes me so angry. Every bereaved mother will have questioned herself a thousand times about whether she is to blame, or whether she could have done something different to save her baby, so for this to be asked is more than insensitive, it is cruel. Most people will never be given a reason for the death of their baby, and that is a bitter pill to swallow. Let us support people, and not fall into the trap of wanting to find a reason for the loss.

'Do you think it's something genetic?'

Who knows, and is it up to you to ask? Again, every parent will ask themselves a million questions, and this is bound to be one of them, but it is a highly personal question and not one to be asked by someone who is trying to offer valuable support.

*'Have you heard about this study or x/y/z information –
it may help you find a reason?'*

I know this comes from a real wish to help, but sadly it's
often not taken in that way, and could be seen as, 'If you
had known about x/y/z, your baby wouldn't have died.'
Most parents who have lost a baby will search for new
studies and reports continually, so if there is fresh data and
information out there, trust me, they will find it themselves.

'Have you thought about having tests?'

Again, this is a pretty personal question and not something
I would recommend asking a bereaved parent.

'It wasn't meant to be'

My instinct is to shout, 'No kidding, Sherlock!' when I hear
this being said. It really does annoy me, as it belittles loss
and disrespects the grieving person.

'Do you think you will keep trying?'

Way too personal a question, and it almost implies that
maybe the couple shouldn't continue to try for a child in
case they have to endure a further loss. Just support them,
rather than making them discuss the future with you.

'Do you not think you have suffered enough?'

Yes, of course, they have suffered enough! One loss is too
much, let alone multiple. However, if someone desperately
wants to have more children, they may – even knowing
more pain could be endured down the line – choose to try

for more children. Having people challenge this decision causes needless suffering.

'Wow, you are putting your family through grief, aren't you?'

I hear this said so often to people who have encountered multiple miscarriages and I find it pretty inexcusable. It means they are not just carrying the pain of loss, but they are also being asked to carry the guilt of others suffering due to their journey to have children.

'But you were so early on, weren't you?'

Another statement that minimises someone's loss and grief. Gestation doesn't change the amount someone grieves; they have lost a baby, that is the only thing that matters. If someone loses a family member who was 48 years old, that doesn't earn them the opportunity to grieve more or less than someone who has lost a person at the age of 50. The same applies with babies and children. Age doesn't matter. Gestation doesn't matter. Are they grieving a loss? If the answer is yes, just support them.

'Do you wish you hadn't told people you were pregnant?'/'Do you wish you had waited until you were in the "safe zone" before telling people you were pregnant?'

Never encourage people to stay silent about pregnancy, or make them feel guilty for sharing their news. The more people who know, the greater the potential support network should they need it.

Also, one of our charity's national campaigns is to encourage people to break the '12-week rule', which counsels keeping schtum until you pass 12 weeks of pregnancy, just in case you lose the baby. This is a very unsubtle way of discouraging people from telling anyone if they encounter loss. People need support when they go through the trauma of baby loss, so the more people who know about the pregnancy, the more likely they are to offer support should the worst happen.

'This is the issue with early pregnancy tests, isn't it? People find out they are pregnant so much earlier on!'

Yes, people do find out they are pregnant much earlier with the invention of the home pregnancy test. And, yes, tests do now tell you about a pregnancy way earlier than ever before – but surely this is a good thing?

Firstly, it's showing the medical world how common baby loss is, and that means more studies are being conducted in this area of medical research. Secondly, it allows people to know their baby existed, even if they didn't stay for long. I know that for me personally, I was so happy to be able to celebrate the fact my babies were here, even though I then had to grieve their departure.

'Is miscarriage just like a heavy period?'

No, it really isn't. Again, it is insulting to anyone who has had a miscarriage for this even to be mentioned or questioned. Not only are the physical symptoms so much greater (for the majority of people), but you also have to deal with the enormous emotional impact of miscarriage, and then the physical recovery post-loss too. It really couldn't be more different from a period and suggesting it is similar is like comparing a tsunami to a gentle wave in the ocean.

'At least you didn't need to, you know, give birth!'

Having a miscarriage is giving birth and so is delivering a stillborn baby. Sometimes there isn't a visible body, depending on gestation, but you are still delivering your child. Again, by minimising the experience a bereaved mother has gone through, you are pouring salt in the wound and certainly not helping recovery.

'I am sure you will have another one!'

Many people who lose a child don't go on to have another child, so how can this be presumed or stated with any certainty. Some people physically can't have more children. Some decide they can't risk further pain or the physical consequence of another pregnancy or delivery. Some people are no longer in a relationship so they have no clue as to how they can even try to conceive another child.

Whatever the circumstances, let's not focus on further children; let's focus all attention on the baby they have lost.

'In a few weeks, you will be like a whole new person!'

Positivity doesn't change the reality, and while you might like to fast-forward time so that the person standing in front of you isn't in pain, you cannot rescue them, and you can't say with all honesty that things will be better soon. By even trying to do this you remove yourself from being a trusted and reliable confidante, as it shows a real lack of empathy and compassion to speak with such authority about something you have no actual knowledge of.

'You are putting your body through it, aren't you!'

I don't believe they are 'putting their body through anything', they are purely wanting to have a child. To imply any responsibility for the fact they are now grieving is cruel.

'Maybe if you didn't think about it, it would be easier'

Grief can't be denied or avoided. In fact, the more you try not to think about it, the more it can overwhelm the brain. It needs time and space to be processed, so by encouraging people to not think about the loss, you are doing them a disservice.

'Perhaps you are dwelling on it too much'

While it is possible to get overly consumed with focusing on loss (which of course wouldn't be healthy), the majority of people aren't dwelling on grief; they are simply trying to survive the loss. Their brain needs time to come to terms with the trauma, and unless they give themselves space to focus on their situation, they will never be able to move forwards healthily. Let me also remind you that there is no 'normal' when it comes to loss, so who can even determine what is 'too much'? Too much to you may not be enough for another person, so we must be mindful not to judge or critique how any person journeys through grief.

'Do you think society over-sentimentalises child loss?'

The moment you ask a grieving parent this you are saying to them, 'Wow, you are making too big a deal out of baby loss, aren't you!' Not only is this deeply hurtful, but it is also demeaning of human life.

'Losing a baby early on in pregnancy is just losing cells, isn't it?'

For some it may be like losing cells; for others, however early they have lost their baby, it was just that, a baby. The only person who should tell you what their baby meant to them is the parents.

'Maybe this is just a sign that you shouldn't be a parent or aren't ready to be a parent'

It is hard to believe that this is ever said to a grieving parent, but I have heard it being uttered, so I know it happens. It's often said to teenage mums, where people feel they have almost been rescued from an unplanned pregnancy, but I have also heard of it being told to parents who have encountered large numbers of miscarriages. It is hurtful, it's thoughtless and should never be thought, let alone voiced.

'Why don't you just embrace life and stop putting your-self through this!'

For some people, all they want to do is have a child. While that can seem odd or confusing to those who may not want children, or to those who don't understand about loss, you have to accept that some people (and that included me) are wanting a child so badly, it is worth risking the pain of loss. Once that ticking clock started, I felt hostage to it. I never believed I was putting myself through anything; I just hoped one day I would have a healthy baby in my arms and a child to raise.

'Aren't you feeling better yet?'

Usually, this question gets asked within two to four weeks post-baby loss – shocking, isn't it? Sadly, if people don't grieve fast, the world often makes you feel abnormal for still hurting, for still crying and for still feeling broken. As soon as you say the words 'aren't you', you are putting an expectation on that person, that they should be further on in their journey, and that brings more hurt and pain to their door. Instead, ask: 'How are you feeling today?' Or: 'Have you been able to experience any moments of peace this week?'

'When do you think you will be back to normal?'

I can answer this one for you. Never. They will never return to the old them. Loss and grief change you for ever, so if you can accept that and then gently help them discover it, you will be an excellent support for someone while they walk through grief.

Proactive Advice for Family and Friends

Having covered what not to say, I would love now to offer you some practical tips on how you can support someone who has lost a child. Prior to being trained and then subsequently working in the field of bereavement care, I remember feeling so confused when I was faced with helping bereaved friends and family members – I wanted to make things better for them, but I didn't know what help to offer. I hope this chapter makes you feel empowered and equipped to support any broken-hearted people on your path through life.

When supporting a loved one, you need to realise that things can stack up and suddenly reach crisis point, so be aware of some of the typical responses:

Wanting to run away: What they want is to escape the pain, and, in their head, they feel like they can run away from it. Sadly, this is not the case, and even if they do travel, the grief goes with them. Listen to them expressing their heart's desire.

Not wanting to leave the house: Often people find security in their home and can almost become phobic about leaving their house, as the world can feel like a terrifying place. Of course, I would not advocate dragging people outside against their will, but I do always recommend gently encouraging people to step out their front door regularly. The longer it is left, the harder it can become to do. Little and often is a right approach.

Panic attacks: Some may have experienced these pre-loss, but for others the loss may have triggered their first attack; either way, it is terrifying for the person. Be aware that this isn't something that can just be brushed off and it is the brain's way of saying, 'I can't cope right now.' Gently encourage them to seek help from a professional and chat with their GP.

Lack of appetite/eating much more than usual: Most of the time, people's appetite will return to normal within a month, so encourage them to take plenty of fluids. Eating little and often is usually more comfortable for those in the depths of grief, and a great gift is lots of snack packs, as nibbling on food can make appetite return. If their regular eating pattern doesn't resume within a month, I will often suggest a person should sit down and talk in depth with a friend or a professional, to see if verbalising their grief helps.

What to Consider

Please don't be scared about seeing pain and grief up close and personal. Yes, it is hard to see someone you care about upset, but if you were in their shoes you would want the people you love to surround you, and you can be one of these people to them.

* Be aware that baby loss can trigger a host of other emotional issues. If someone has issues in his or her marriage/relationship, they are likely to surface at this

time. Similarly, if a person has issues with their parents or siblings, these are likely to come to a breaking point at this time of emotional crisis.

* Seek to understand more about loss and grief if you haven't personally experienced it. It is easy to oversimplify loss and almost consider it unnatural, but it is one of the most natural parts of life; there is a time to be born and a time to die. If you can become comfortable talking about the subject of death, you will be able to support the grieving much better.

* Don't presume anger is part of grief. Of course, some people may experience a degree of anger in the grieving process; however, many won't, and to assume someone's anger is just part of grief can be harmful to the individual and mean injustices aren't addressed. I support many people whose babies' deaths could have been prevented. Often those around them, and even some health professionals, disregard their claims and stories by saying, 'They are in the anger stage of grief and need to aim it somewhere.' We need to listen to people at all times, and we need to hear their stories without presumption or assumption, and if someone is angry, let's find out why.

* Think before you share. When you are bereaved, some information is more painful to hear. For example, 'Hey, I'm expecting a baby' can be a kick in the guts to someone who just miscarried, so be mindful of this. If you do have a pregnancy announcement, tell them ideally before you make the news public, and ensure they don't hear it via social media. The best way often is to write it on a card, as this means the person isn't put on the spot and can process what you have told them before responding. Grief can make people less patient for a time and also

blunter, so think and be mindful. This doesn't mean you shouldn't share about your life at all. I welcomed news of other life issues or situations when I was grieving; it gave me time to think of someone else, but how it was shared was significant.

* Know and accept they are likely to be tired most of the time. Grief is exhausting; it uses every bit of the physical and mental energy available to a person, and often that means they spend a lot of their time saying how tired they are. Reassure them that that is normal, and when you see them or do activities together, perhaps focus on things that don't need much physical energy.

* Often bereaved people will tell you they forget things all the time and find it difficult to focus; this is just because their brain is in overdrive dealing with the pain of loss. Think of it like a computer having a hundred tabs open on the browser – everything slows down, and sometimes the whole PC needs to shut down and reboot. Offer gentle reminders to those you are supporting to alleviate the pressure, even if it's just by sending a simple text – for instance, 'Looking forward to seeing you tomorrow at 1pm.' Then you aren't highlighting the fact they may not have remembered the arrangement or the time.

* It is okay to laugh and smile. One of the things that the bereaved struggle with is allowing themselves to smile without feeling guilty, as they fear those around them will assume they are 'over the loss' if they laugh. It can also feel disloyal to the person they have lost to smile and enjoy life. I spend my life reassuring the bereaved that it's not only okay to smile, but it's also crucial that they do, as the brain can only handle so much trauma, and it needs light relief and an escape at times.

* Children and babies. For some, children are hard to be around post-loss, for others (and I fit into this category) they bring them hope and relief. Every time I saw a baby, a child or even a pregnancy bump, I thought, it can go well for me as it did/has for them – they were like rays of hope wherever I looked. For others it brings pain, and every pregnancy bump they see feels like a slap in the face. The only person who can tell you how they feel is the bereaved person, so ask them. Let them set the agenda here; if they prefer only to see non-pregnant people or babies for a time, that is their choice. Nothing you say will change how they feel, so even if you disagree with how they may handle it, be kind, gentle and non-judgemental. Whatever helps them survive their journey of loss is a good thing – remember that!

What to Say

Remember, showing up is ultimately what matters. Don't be so afraid of saying the wrong thing that you hide away and say nothing at all. I would much rather have someone say something than someone who ignores my suffering.

* Let the bereaved set the tone and the agenda rather than presuming. Let them say if they feel happy, sad, confused or lost. If they control the dialogue, it ensures what you say is appropriate to how they feel in that moment.
* Ask in-depth questions, not just surface ones.

It is easy to stick to 'safe' questions; for example, 'How are you doing?' However, most of the time people will have become so practised at answering these that they answer before they even think, and will reply, 'Coping, thanks' or 'I'm okay, thanks.' By going just a little broader and reframing questions, you can properly engage with people who need to talk about their pain. How about asking:

* 'What was your most difficult moment to navigate this week?'
* 'Did you find joy in anything this week?'
* 'Was there anything you needed this week that I could have helped you with?'

Pay close attention to their response. If they respond openly, that's great. If they don't, spend time thinking about how better to phrase a question for the next time you see them. Prior preparation can make you feel more confident in your interaction, and once you have truly engaged them in conversation, you won't need to say much as the bereaved person will do most of the talking.

* Ask if they have named their baby and, if they have, talk about them by name, and refer to them by name in general conversation. It won't upset them; it will show them you care!
* Ask questions about their experience of birth/loss. People are often desperate to share their stories (even if they do shed copious amounts of tears in the process). Of course, some of these may be hard to hear, but some will also be beautiful. Believe me when I say that every time you sit and listen to a bereaved person's story, you are giving them a real gift.

What to Do

Most people will rush to support those grieving in the couple of weeks immediately following a loss, but this often then dwindles or stops altogether. People naturally go back to their typical day-to-day lives and presume the bereaved person has moved on too. But they won't have; they are just as heartbroken, and are often now left with little or no support. Be aware of this and increase your support in the weeks that follow, rather than reducing it.

* Ensure they have details of the support available to them. People have to want support and reaching out for it is the first part of their healing process.
* Do things that show the bereaved person you are thinking of them, even if you can't see them face to face (at all or daily/weekly). Send them notes, text messages, cards, gifts. A book can be a helpful gift so that, if and when they feel they need help or assistance, it will already be at their fingertips.
* Make a note in your diary of key anniversaries and reach out to the bereaved in the weeks before the date to say, 'I am thinking of you, leading up to x anniversary' – this means the world to grieving people. Then also reach out to them on the day, even if you only send a card. Then it is just as important to contact them a few weeks after and ask them how they coped.
* Offer practical help at home. Try to be more specific than saying, 'Call me if you need help.' Instead try: 'Are you okay with me bringing dinner over for the next few weeks?' Or, 'Can I stock your freezer with ready-made meals so that when you have no desire to cook or even

eat, there is food there for you?' Or, 'Can I come and vacuum, clean or do your ironing?' When you are struggling to survive the weight of grief, household chores are the last thing on a person's mind, and if you can help make their living environment a nicer or tidier space, that is a gift. When you spend a lot of time crying on the bathroom floor, it being clean is a blessing.

* If the bereaved person has other children, offer to help take care of them. While it is good for children to see that grief and loss are part of life, and that crying is okay and indeed healthy, they also have a limit on how much they can tolerate. If you can take them out, and allow them to have times of fun and joy amid the sorrow, that can be helpful for the parents. I know that when we lost Samuel, my sister Hayley coming and playing with our daughter Esme also gave Andy and I the time to chat, reflect and the space to weep together.

* Offer physical touch if appropriate. Now, this comes with a warning, as some people hate physical touch and will avoid it at all costs, so only make physical contact if you know the person well enough to be sure they will welcome it. Touch is important when offering compassion and empathy because it can make people feel heard and loved. Just holding their hand or hugging them can make them feel safer, grounded and cared for.

* Arrange meetings/hang-outs where they will feel at ease being real. Many people aren't naturally comfortable at dinner parties at the best of times, and events like this are even harder when you feel bereft, so try to create more casual and relaxed opportunities, so they don't feel a need to put on a 'brave face'. Please also be mindful of holding more formal events and not inviting the bereaved

person, as that can cause real hurt. So, yes, you may need to change how you do things for a few months, but if it helps the grieving person, surely it's worth it?

* Be flexible with plans. Make it clear you are fine if the arrangements change right up to the last minute. Often what stops people who are grieving making plans is that they are worried they may suddenly not feel able to go out, which means it feels safer to them not to make any arrangements with anyone for fear of letting others down. By giving them permission always to change, cancel or move events, you will provide them with the peace of mind they need to take the risk. If/when the person does change arrangements, be sure never to make them feel guilty or to look put out, even if you have to do a fantastic acting job. (Yes, I know you are human too, so may feel disappointed if the day at the spa is cancelled an hour before you were due to leave, hence my acting suggestion . . .)

* Be forgiving and patient. When journeying through grief, it can mean a person feels so overwhelmed and numb, they stop being thoughtful or kind. They may appear emotionless or too emotional. They may be brutal in their responses and lack sensitivity in how they phrase things. They may not ask how your day went or for news on your work promotion. I beg of you to accept that this isn't personal, and it does not mean the bereaved person has become selfish and self-centred. It just says they are crawling through life right now, and they are so overwhelmed with pain their typical responses to things are on hold. Give them time, and they will start asking about you again; it won't always be about them.

5

Layers of Grief

You may have read many articles and leaflets on grief and loss, which allude to the fact that there are set stages. These are usually:

* Denial
* Anger
* Bargaining
* Depression
* Acceptance

While these can be accurate for some, people who go through grief via these steps, in this set order, will definitely be in the minority. Grief is not that straightforward.

It may be easier to talk about myself when explaining this. Once I was told my babies had 100 per cent been confirmed as dead, I didn't deny they had passed away. I never felt any anger about their deaths, not anger at myself or the hospital, or my family. None, no anger at all. I then didn't bargain. I didn't have depression. However, I did get acceptance. I would say my stages of grief looked more like this.

* Shocked
* Scared
* Shocked
* Confused
* Lost
* Acceptance

Every person's steps will be unique to them, even if there are strong common themes or similarities with those of others.

Grief really can come off in layers – one minute you can be fine and the next you are crying, and this can happen over years or even over a lifetime. Society tells us everything has a time limit, and that is a strongly held belief when it comes to grief. The sad part of this is that it means most people grieve in silence. This is especially true if a person didn't feel able to process their grief at the time of their loss. If years later they allow themselves time to process the pain, society often doesn't respect and acknowledge how vital this is to a person's well-being, and can make them feel shame for expressing their pain and sadness so long after the loss has happened.

When we launched the Mariposa Trust and the Saying Goodbye Remembrance Services, we initially thought they would be for recently bereaved people, but we were so wrong. They have been happening now for many years, and every single service is made up of people who have lost recently, as well as people who lost their babies 40, 50, 60, 70 years ago.

Grief is a long journey; it will be patient and travel with a person until they are ready or able to process it.

A short while ago, I was talking to my friend one evening and she was telling me how she couldn't stop crying and how her grief for the babies she had lost many years ago suddenly felt fresh and raw again. This new layer of grief was triggered by her youngest son leaving for university. Nothing could have prepared her for this wave to hit, as she had never lived through the experience of suddenly having no children residing at home. I asked Siobhan if she could explain the pain, and this is what she said.

Siobhan's Story

It took me ten pregnancies to get my three sons. The miscarriages ranged from early to late-gestation losses and each of the losses threads through my very being. I have got to the stage of my grief where I have accepted the losses and use my experience to help others in my daily work. Or so I thought.

If my last losses had survived the pregnancies, my children would now be 15, 14 and 11. My youngest live son is 18 and I proudly sent him off to university in September, the third of the brothers to go in three years. As his survival was a miracle and he nearly died at birth due to my blood-clotting disorder, the pride is even more enormous at his achievement.

The joy I feel at how well my three sons are all doing at university is accentuated each day when we chat on the phone about how their day has been. So the ferocity of the 'empty-nest syndrome' was unexpected to say the least. I miss my boys, but it was so much more than that. The truth is that my home should not be child-free; it should still have children here if they had not died, and this grief is overwhelming. I feel that I have lost them all over again and that grief is raw and painful.

Maybe having live children tempered the grief I experienced through all the losses and what I am experiencing now is more real. Although what I feel now seems sadly familiar – the tears, physical heartache, the nightmares and waking up crying and shouting out are things I thought I had left behind. I find myself imagining my lost children in the empty spaces left by their university-student brothers.

So I don't know how to cope with this grief, as although it feels familiar I am struggling with finding a way out of it due to the unexpectedness of it all. I feel I am back to square one, but this time there is one crucial difference. I know I have a support system around me who understand the grief and I am now not alone as a grieving mother.

These layers can be revealed at any time, and you can't prepare for it; all you can do is not be scared of it when it shows its face. If you don't fight it, or resist processing the pain that surfaces, the tears will settle, and the grief will quickly soften again so it becomes easier to carry. Grief is like an onion made up of many, many layers. These layers of 'grief' can be revealed at any time.

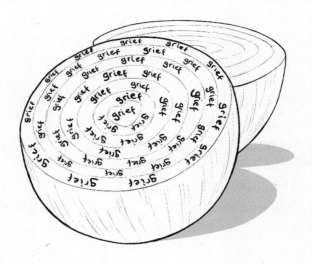

Healing

This is a difficult subject to explore but I know I need to include it in this book as I am asked about it constantly. 'Do people heal post losing a baby?' The answer is some do, and some don't.

I guess we need to decipher what I mean by 'heal'. To me, not healing means someone feels: despair. Hopelessness. Physical and mental torture about the loss. Being constantly unhappy.

I don't feel those things any more, which is why I feel my heart has healed. I fully accept that my five babies didn't survive, and I have come to terms with the pain of losing them. There will always be parts of me missing, as I have five little ones not sitting here in my home, and that will never be 'okay', but I also feel blessed they were here at all. Probably, most importantly, I have gone on to be happier than I ever was pre-loss in their honour.

Will I always talk about them? YES! They are as much my children as my living children here with me are, so of course I will talk about them, celebrate them and smile when I think about them.

Do I miss them? *Yes, desperately.*

Do I wish they hadn't died? *Yes, of course, I long for them to be here with me.*

Do I have times where grief can hit me out of nowhere and I have a cry? *Yes! Very rarely, but I still have those times.*

Does it hurt to talk about the babies I lost? *No, not at all. I love talking about all my children, and the experience of losing them is now part of my story and I feel totally comfortable talking about every detail of it.*

So why do some people not heal? This is pretty impossible to answer, as everyone is unique, but I think I can unravel some of the myths surrounding it. If someone doesn't heal, does it mean they loved their child more than someone else whose heart has healed? No, of course it doesn't. Love and healing aren't linked.

The reason I knew I needed to address this in my book is that so many people ask me every week how I have found a path of total joy to walk down, following such loss. They want to know how they can experience the same, and how they can use the grief they have experienced to embrace life more. The reason I have shared my story publicly is to try to bring hope to people who are desperate, to be a light when people are crawling around in the dark, and I would never want anyone to think that as soon as they lose a baby they are doomed to an unhappy life, as it's not always like that for everyone.

I would like to say that having a healed heart does not mean that people won't at times feel broken, or feel acute pain, or feel grief-stricken and freshly bereaved. This is sadly part of grief and the walk of grief takes a life-time.

Can we make people heal? No we can't. Everyone's walk is unique to them. Some start on the path weeks after loss;

for others it's years, for some it may take decades, and for some it sadly never happens.

When my heart started to mend, I knew it would be a very different shape from what it had been before, and that was okay. In fact, that was better, as I wanted loss to have changed me. My heart was now bigger than ever, because the love for my children had expanded its capacity, so a new shape was a good thing.

Are there obstacles that can make healing harder for some people? Yes, there are:

Personality: How we journey through loss and life in general can be shaped by our personality and character traits.

Upbringing: How we are raised, and the skills we have developed through life experiences, definitely play a part in how we recover from trauma and loss.

Lack of joy: If a person's life has no hope within it, or they have nothing to look forward to in the future, recovery from trauma and loss is more challenging.

To recap:

* I was broken
* My heart was rebuilt in a different shape from before
* I am no longer broken, my heart did heal, but I am for ever changed

How I started on the path to healing my heart:

* I kept talking about the loss and my experiences – talking is key to the brain and heart accepting what has

happened, and it helps any trauma connected to the loss(es) to be processed.

* I gave myself permission to visit the pain whenever I felt it was needed – I didn't run from it or deny it was there; I was willing to face it head-on.

* I spoke about my children – they were not a secret or a taboo, and that meant I could process the grief, and other people then felt equally comfortable talking about them around me.

* I refused to accept the world's standpoint that gestation plays a part in a person's worth, and because of this I never felt a need to justify my children's existence. While you are constantly needing to defend a person's worth, it is really hard to heal, as you end up becoming a campaigner rather than a grieving parent.

* I stopped trying to recover and to move through grief faster. You simply can't rush grief and the more you try, the slower you journey through it. If you can lay down all your expectations and just go at your own pace, grieving becomes a much easier process.

* I stopped trying to be happy again. I decided that to be happy in the immediate aftermath was out of my reach, so I decided to just live to make others happy. By doing this I unexpectedly rediscovered my smile and joy.

* I re-engaged with life. By joining in things with your family, friends and community you see that life can bring you happy moments again, and, while this is hard to accept at first, it makes life more tolerable moving forwards.

* I started to look after myself again. In the initial part of the grieving process I stopped caring about what I looked like; in fact, the worse I looked, the better I felt,

as I felt the outside then showed a glimmer of what I was feeling like on the inside. After some time, I decided to start taking care of myself again, and, while it felt like an effort initially, it made me feel more like me again and that helped in the long run.

* I engaged with others who had experienced similar loss, and hearing that many of my experiences were shared by them helped me feel less alone.

This is my walk. This is my path. Your path will be unique to you. How you heal is personal to you, and nothing is wrong and nothing is right in the way you journey your way through grief. I do encourage you to be fearless in addressing the pain; don't run from the grief, face it head-on.

We cannot ever judge another grieving person, or critique how they heal, or don't heal; all we can do is cheer them on and help them on their walk. I hope explaining how I have healed helps you in some way. Losing a person you love in no way means you are automatically doomed to be sad for ever – this is what I needed to hear, and so I wanted to tell you.

The Quest for Happiness

I spent endless nights wailing on the floor, repeating over and over, 'I just want to be happy again – someone tell me how to be happy.' Losing my sense of happiness was probably a major layer of my grief pie. I had always considered myself a truly happy, joy-filled person, and to have this suddenly removed from me felt like I lost my identity. I didn't recognise this sad, heartbroken person staring back at me in the mirror. The eyes that used to shine with expectation and excitement now looked lifeless and terrified – who was I without a smile on my face?

I guess this is when my quest to discover what happiness truly meant began. Maybe true happiness could still be found following heartbreak and loss; maybe, just maybe, I could still be happy, even in the depths of grief – perhaps one can still be in mourning and still be a happy person?

So, what did this quest look like in practical terms? I started by acknowledging all the beautiful things I still had in my life. I won't bore you with listing them here, as your list would be unique to you and comparison helps no one. But we all have something to be grateful for. Perhaps it is your partner, your soulmate; maybe it's having lots of friends to support you, or one special friend who has been able to carry you through tragedy – whatever or whoever you include on your list, just by taking time to consider how blessed you are to have them in your life can tweak your negative perspective on life, and it definitely changed mine.

I chose not to say, 'Why me?' Instead I said, 'Why not me?' This stopped me feeling victimised by life, and made me face the fact that these terrible things happen to many people (too many people), and I wasn't being singled out. It wasn't because I deserved it, or that life was picking on me – it's simply the nature of loss and grief; it doesn't discriminate, it targets anyone and everyone.

I decided to let go of the deep desperation to feel happy again – the more I talked about the loss of my joy and the more I dissected why I couldn't be happy again, the sadder I felt. I had to choose to let it go, and say if I am never happy again, then that is okay. Is it what I desired? No. Would I like it to be different? Yes. But longing for it doesn't bring it back.

Next, I decided to read about people who had overcome tragedy. I soaked up every story I could find about those who had been broken by life, but had somehow continued on. This stopped me feeling sorry for myself and made me look in awe at these amazing people who are dotted around the globe. People who you would think should be rocking in a corner, but who are instead leading meaningful lives. I saw how loss had transformed their souls – and I made a choice to be one of these people. That didn't mean I needed to do something extraordinary, or build the world's biggest orphanage, it just meant I wasn't going to let loss destroy my future; I was going to find hope in the darkness. I noticed that none of these beautiful humans talked much about happiness – as happiness was a small emotion compared to what they were feeling and expressing. Anything can make you happy, and happiness is a transient state and emotion. Being fulfilled, hope-filled, compassionate, empathetic and a good human are all way more important.

I said to Andy that we needed to do something for people who are desperate and unhappy right now. It didn't matter what it was, but I needed to know that what we did would help someone feel cared for. We chose to make hampers for people who were alone and lonely, massive hampers that would feed them for weeks. It was a big task and took us weeks to do – but boy did it feel good to know people wouldn't be going hungry, and also would feel loved. Then we put together rucksacks for people who are homeless – these included sleeping bags, socks, wet wipes, mints, notepad and pens, tissues, toothbrushes and so much more. We then handed them to groups working with homeless people across two cities. Again, this took us weeks – but we felt like we were doing something to help other people and I can't tell you how good that felt. It didn't matter that we were sobbing while putting these packs together; we did it anyway, and we knew our pain was being ploughed into helping other people. These are just two of the many things we did, and I can wholeheartedly recommend you do something that removes you from your own pain for a short amount of time, and makes you look at the wider world. (My only word of caution here is: don't volunteer for things and not follow through; charities have so few resources and when people let them down it really affects them. Also, don't offer to do anything that means you need to provide emotional support – wait until your heart has mended to do that.)

A massive milestone then happened: I gave myself permission to feel joy again. Me smiling didn't mean I didn't love my babies, and it didn't mean I wasn't hurting any more. So I watched as much stand-up comedy as I could. I watched Nigella cooking delicious food, Oprah conducting inspiring interviews and *The Vicar of Dibley* on repeat on TV. If it was going to make me laugh or smile, or bring me any enjoyment, I said, 'Yes, please, bring it on.'

I then wrote down how I was feeling, on notepads, in journals, anywhere I could find space to express my feelings. Pain needs a voice at times, and if we can let it flow out of us in words, it can help the brain accept the circumstances one now lives in.

I explored my faith more. Some find faith through loss, some reject it, and others go deeper into it. I was already a committed Christian, and I have to say that having a faith really did help me, way more than I could say in just one paragraph. I think loss often makes people look into the meaning of life, or other deep life issues, and I completely understand why, as you just feel so small and insignificant. My faith helped me as it made me look beyond this world, and while this world seemed full of pain that was a much-needed respite.

Next, I stopped delaying my happiness with thoughts such as: 'If x happens, I will feel happy again. If y and z happen, I will find my peace.' It was time to stop postponing things and making excuses for why I couldn't feel it. I could feel happy right now if I chose to – even in the depths of my darkness. I could be a happy person and a broken person.

I discovered that whenever I said I will carry my babies in my heart for ever, this was clinically correct, and I can't tell you how much this helped me. Most people are unaware that every child a woman carries actually changes her DNA – how amazing is that? Science has shown that cells of every child remain in the woman's body, whether that baby died *in utero* or at birth, or if the child lived.

Over time, it then happened. Not in a way I imagined it to happen. I wanted to be as happy as I was pre-loss, and to my surprise I was now happier than I had been before losing my babies. (I felt this before having a living child to raise – so it's not dependent on having a child to raise.) Life had more meaning. The depth of pain I had experienced created new, much deeper reserves in my soul (and, yes, it scared me that a human could feel that much sorrow), but post-loss those reserves could be filled with joy, and as they were now way deeper they could hold so much more happiness.

I can't promise you this is a foolproof way to rediscover happiness; all I can say is this is how I found mine again. If any of this helps lead you to the path to find your smile, I will be delighted.

15 Questions

I am always amazed at the diverse questions that I get asked at events and on social media, and I thought it might be helpful to include some of my favourites here as they may give you an insight into my thinking and stance on life.

1. What shocked you about grief?

Many, many things. I may have trained as a counsellor prior to experiencing loss, but nothing in the world could have prepared me for walking the path I did.

* One thing that surprised me was that my heart wasn't just broken because of the loss of my baby; my heart also broke due to the mammoth disappointment I was carrying, and due to the terror of the unknown. The agony was kind of surreal, and it made me feel like I had left the planet and had transcended to a different universe.
* I was shocked at the million questions that rushed around my brain. The: 'What if you don't survive this?' 'What if you are broken for ever?' 'What if you never stop crying?' 'What if you never have a child to raise?'

Oh, the questions, the never-ending questions of a brain that seems to seek to destroy you when you are deeply broken. I found the only way to survive this was not to torture myself with seeking the answers; I simply kept telling myself the same thing on repeat: ' . . . Then I will survive it.' I gave in to the pain, I submitted to the questions that only grief born from deep love can birth and, over time, the questions stopped – but nothing could have prepared me for this part of grief.

* I was so shocked at the immense fear I experienced. Grief really does throw you into a huge black pit. C. S. Lewis said, 'nothing prepared me for the fact that grief looks so like fear'. And boy does that quote ring true. Grief does look so like terror; it is daunting and all-consuming. I feared everything. I feared waking up each morning as I knew I would have to live through another day of fresh pain. I feared going to sleep because of the nightmares. Often when you have a bad dream you wake up and reassure yourself that it is just a dream and nothing to be scared of, but during that time I would wake up and realise the nightmare was real, it was true life – that really terrified me.

* The most shocking thing was that the blackest grief, the haunting, harrowing, please-kill-me-now type of grief, did end. For a long time I didn't think it would, but it did. It gradually changed and became less and less. I would no longer say I am mourning. Whilst I am fully aware grief is a lifelong passage, I don't feel broken any longer. In fact, I feel more whole than I have ever been, and happier than ever – I never believed that was possible in the aftermath of loss.

2. What was the worst part of loss for you (other than losing your child, of course)?

I think one of the worst parts was feeling like the pain was infinite. There was no end in sight, and that is a truly hard thing to live with. The most harrowing part of loss was knowing that however long I waited and however many tears I wept, my child was never coming back. Over time I was able to accept that, while their physical presence here with me was very limited, the love I carried for them was never-ending, and that meant they will always be part of me, and that helped ease the pain.

3. Where did you find strength?

My strength came when I said I will no longer run from this pain. I faced the battle; with shaking legs and a quivering lip, I said I will not hide from the agony, I will process it. Even if that meant wailing on the floor in a pool of tears.

To be expected to face another day on this planet while carrying the weight of grief on your shoulders is similar to being asked to reside in a lion's cage. Daunting, terrifying and incomprehensible – I totally get that, I have been there. And to need to find any kind of strength when you feel broken is pretty impossible, so I tell everyone not even to look for it. Your only task is to take one step forwards today; you don't need to find any hidden reserve – strength will find you, if you don't find it. Whether it finds you in that pool of tears in the valley, or while you are walking on a mountain top – wherever you may be, it will sneak up on you, I promise you.

I also want to say that while I was waiting for strength to find me, I found me!

4. How did you feel ready to move on with life?

If I always waited until I felt mentally or emotionally ready for things, I promise you I would do nothing. My secret? I show up, however I feel.

I also decided very early on that I would never ask, 'Why is this happening to me?' I always thought, 'Why shouldn't this be happening to me.' This stopped me feeling like a victim of circumstance. I also decided to learn from everything – to constantly look for a hidden lesson, or a gift or a blessing, even in the deepest of traumas (which, believe me, isn't easy). I can hand-on-heart say this was a big game-changer for me, as it made me look more positively at things.

5. How did you discover your calling in life?

I have always loved the things that other people forget. As a child, I decided to rescue every slug from our garden. I had seen my parents trying to eliminate them from the flowerbeds (and as a child I couldn't grasp the reason why). I saw that the slugs had babies, and so went on a mission to save this unwanted community. I secretly built a slug village, with shells and pots for them to hide under. I would even take them food each day. Before long all the slugs were safe (and *gulp* breeding). Don't get me wrong, I did not love these slimy creatures. In fact, if they went near me I screamed, but my heart felt so sad that they were being wiped out and no one was speaking up for them. I guess this is when I first glimpsed my calling – to speak for those who struggle to be heard, and to seek out those that are unwanted in society or are marginalised for whatever reason. I am very glad I have moved on from slugs, though!

Having walked through grief after losing five babies, I saw that the broken-hearted are definitely hidden in society, and are mostly forgotten. People find it hard to witness pain, and this can be for many reasons: For some, it may be because it breaks their heart to see others cry. For others, they may see weeping as a weakness. Of course, there are a host of other reasons, too – but collectively they add up to society encouraging people to hide their pain, and they are therefore afraid to be real and authentic about their suffering.

I see it as my job to scream it from the rooftops that sadness is as valid an emotion as joy, and if we refuse to allow people to process and express their pain, we deny them the chance to ever experience true happiness. As a society, we need to come together and rally around those who are being forgotten – the bereaved, the marginalised and the people who are often not heard in this increasingly noisy world.

I have shared my slug rescue as I want to inspire you to look at what sets your heart on fire and to discover your heart's mission, as you can find real purpose in life by learning that.

6. Do you like paving the way?

I believe some people see a path already cleared and think, 'Great – that is the way I need to walk.' I see the wild bracken and thorn-filled forest just next to that nice clear path, and think, 'Wow – I should go in that direction and clear the way, as there may be hidden beauty there.' So if that means I like paving a way, I guess I do, yes.

I never take the easy path; it is kind of against my DNA. To be honest, I sometimes dislike that part of me, as it certainly makes life more complicated, but it also makes life exciting, and it means I create and develop new things constantly.

7. What do you wish someone had told you when you were going through grief?

* Grief can make you hide in the shadows, but it helps to lean into the light. I was so scared to show the real me, the broken me, and it often felt easier to hide that pain away. But if we courageously choose to be vulnerable and let the light hit our faces, we can crawl through the valley of darkness much more easily. Often, we find others who are also crawling, and these people can become lifelong friends – I call them 'valley friends'. They have walked the same path, or perhaps dragged themselves along the same path, and they are usually the people who understand you the most.

* The pain is not limited, as the love is endless. Knowing this would have helped me understand and accept the pain I was going through.

* You don't need to fight to survive. I often used to scream that I couldn't make it through another day, and I didn't want to live a moment longer with the raw agony that only loss can bring. After some time, I discovered I didn't need to fight the pain; the only thing I needed to do was open my eyes when I woke up and bravely look at the

heartbreak and refuse to run from it. To have been told this would have helped me a lot.

* There will be days when you are hit by a fresh wave of grief and you will doubt how far you have swum in the ocean of mourning. Let me reassure you that these waves are part of the journey, they won't put you back. In fact, they do the exact opposite; they carry you forwards if you don't fight them – just hold on to your lifering and let the current carry you on. You won't drown and you may need to tell yourself this a hundred times a day. Let it become your mantra: 'I won't drown; I am just learning to swim.'

* When walking through grief, feelings change by the hour – heck, let's be even more realistic, they change by the second. So, if someone asks you if you are okay now, that doesn't mean you need to be okay in 60 minutes, or that you were okay yesterday. Just try to stay as present as you can.

* Grief isn't something you can control. I think a huge misconception about grief is that it is controllable, that people can choose when and where to feel it and process it, and before losing my babies I probably believed this a little too, if I am honest. Once you have experienced grief first-hand you can only laugh at this myth. Can you control love? No, of course you can't; love is a powerful force that controls people, and the same applies to grief, and we must respect that. Knowing this would have helped me no end.

* Sometimes all the explaining in the world won't help others understand loss and grief. People will always view things from their own level of perception and from their own personal experience.

8. What is your biggest regret surrounding the time of your losses?

* I don't have many, and I am grateful for that. But one big one is that I wish I had told everyone I was pregnant the moment I found out. I robbed myself and my friends and family of that joy. I will never get those opportunities back and I do deeply regret not sharing the news of the pregnancies.
* Another regret is that I wish I had buried all of my babies. Again, something I cannot change now, but I would love to be able to visit one place where all my babies are buried together.

9. Did grief bring you any gifts?

* Grief made me rip up the rule book. Suddenly I got to just be me. I stopped wanting to conform and please those around me. Maybe I was beyond caring? Perhaps I was so broken I felt no shame in sobbing on the floor? Whatever the case, it brought me a freedom to be truly authentic and that really is a gift.
* My babies were robbed of all their tomorrows, but because of them I embrace all of my todays – that is a gift.
* It's in the brokenness . . .
  It's in the waiting . . .
  It's in the pain . . .
  It's in the darkest of places . . .
  that we discover the depth of the love we are able to feel. That is a gift.

10. Why does grief make people feel out of control?

We all like to control our destiny and there is nothing more out of our control than grief. It's not possible for us to predict or defer death, and as such we can't stop grief from entering our lives. Grief brings with it chaos. It collects every element of our lives, puts it all into a big basket and then shakes it.

Things may break in that basket, things will certainly change shape, and the pieces will always come out in a strange and confusing order! No part of this picture is okay for humans.

Many assume grief needs to be conquered, but, actually, it is something people need to face and not fight. This takes a real leap of faith and a complete release of control. It takes real trust to let it surround you like fog on a mountain top, but eventually a path will open up before you and you can step straight through it.

11. What would you say to someone who is trying to stop a family member or friend from crying?

* When you see someone crying, please remember tears have a voice. That voice is so rarely listened to; it is mostly ignored and told to stay quiet for fear of inducing more weeping. But something magical happens if we listen. Those droplets of water speak the profound truth, and tell life-changing stories – so listen to those teardrops.
* To have someone catch every tear is a beautiful gift – you can give that gift to a bereaved person.
* It's easy to sit on the shoreline and judge those swimming

in the ocean of grief, but unless you have nearly drowned at sea, say nothing more than 'Can I send help to you?' or 'How can I help you?' – never 'Perhaps you should stop crying'.

* I think the world can wrongly think it helps others to try to look for a bright side even in tragedy. But sometimes there isn't a bright side, however much people want there to be. Sometimes it's just crap. Agonisingly painful. Overwhelmingly terrible – and we just have to accept that, and give people the freedom to sob.
* Sometimes people just need to be lifted on to another's shoulders so they can see over the parapet of grief. Your shoulders may be good for that.
* Remember, grief is sacred; it is liquid love streaming from the cracks of a broken heart. Please don't fear it.

12. What do you want people to know about grieving parents?

* That most parents want their children's names written on every single page of their life story. Bereaved parents frequently feel pressured not to talk of the children they have lost, because society wants to avoid mentioning them by name. It's as if parents are being forced to rip out the pages of their story. But as bereaved parents we want our children to be celebrated (however long their life was within the womb or outside of it). You can help this happen by talking about these precious children and by not fearing the subject of loss.
* People often focus on the physical pain of loss, and while this can of course be huge, if you ask any parent they will tell you the physical pain is minuscule compared

to the earth-shattering emotional pain that feels never-ending. So perhaps focus on the emotional pain that both parents are suffering with.

* Be aware that it is pretty hard to articulate the pain. Most people are taught the language to express joy, but there are rarely lessons in how to communicate devastating loss. I had no clue how to express that my world was unravelling in front of my eyes, and most people are the same. Give people time and space to find the words they need to convey their experience. Sometimes they may be so numb and overwhelmed with grief that the only thing they are able to do is sit and stare at a wall. In those moments, all they need is for you to sit and stare at the wall with them.

* People crave normality and often want to do normal everyday things without fear of judgement.

* If everyone surrounding those bereaved recognises the loss, it means the individual/couple can focus on grieving, rather than utilising their small reserves of energy to defend their right to grieve.

* That when a couple lose a baby it is not only a story of pain; there is also beauty in the ashes. The painful truth for me was that I was never going to get the chance to raise my lost babies, but I am glad there was a time when I believed I would, as those moments filled me with unbridled joy, and I will always cherish that time.

* If a family goes on to have more children the ultimate challenge for some is to come to a sweet acceptance and peace that the child in their arms may not be here if the child they have lost hadn't died. I get asked how to deal with this many times each week and my answer is always the same. Life is unbearably complex and

everything doesn't need to make sense. Sometimes we won't know why things happen, and why some have had to say goodbye before others can say hello, but we don't need to torture ourselves with the questions. We can just love the ones we have lost and love the ones here with us.

13. What tips can you offer to those experiencing feelings of jealousy towards pregnant people?

This is something I am asked about countless times each week, so if you are feeling jealous of pregnancy bumps, or finding it hard to engage with babies, please know you are not alone. Let me also reassure you that you are not a bad or unkind person if you are wrestling with these emotions. I would say this is high on the list of things people struggle with most post-loss, especially in the first 12 months. Most people beg me to help them switch off these feelings, as they also feel incredible guilt for having them, so it's a double burden. Sadly, there is no cast-iron way to stop the thoughts or feelings from surfacing; you just have to process your grief and hope your feelings then realign.

What I found personally helpful was to try to see every pregnancy bump as a beacon of light. My thinking was: if they can carry a baby to term, so can I. Likewise, whenever I saw a baby (and we all know you see babies everywhere following loss) I used to think that if that baby can survive, so can mine.

14. How can people help their living children cope with baby loss?

Children are so resilient and my best advice is to be honest and open. We have comprehensive advice on the saying-goodbye.org website, and that includes a film we made with Dr Ranj that you can sit down and watch with a child, so head there for more information.

15. What words would you whisper into a bereaved parent's ear today?

Maybe today you are looking at people on Instagram or Facebook, or at others in your life, and thinking, 'How? How on earth have they got to the stage in life where they are happy? How have they run the race and are still here to tell the tale?' Well, let me reassure you of this:

I had no clue how I was going to get to the finish line. I didn't even know how I was going to get over the starting line, but I just kept stepping forwards and, before I knew it, I was on my way. So, I am here to cheer you on and be that small voice you need to hear telling you, 'You can do this and you will survive.'

PART 2

60 Days of Support and Journalling

DAY 1

* *

Wanting to hide away following mind-blowing grief is not just expected, it is totally normal. It doesn't mean you are having a breakdown, or have suddenly developed a panic disorder; it simply means you need time out, and time to process what you have just experienced. So be gentle with yourself. Allow the tears to fall, eat chocolate, eat comforting soup, do whatever you need to do to survive in the aftermath.

TASK FOR THE DAY

Write here how you feel. Be honest. Be raw. This is your space to process your feelings.

It's understandable that you choose to hide
under your duvet.

It is totally fine to slip down a wall, screaming
and shouting that life isn't fair.

It is okay that you stand in the shower with tears
streaming down your face faster than the jets
of water spraying your body.

Grief hurts.

Loss is mind-blowing.

Heartbreak is earth-shattering.

Whatever you need to do to survive is FINE.

ZOË CLARK-COATES

DAY 2

* *

Self-care. It is normal not to want to look after yourself following loss, but I urge you to ignore the desire to forget you, because *you* matter. Often people see little purpose in eating well, or trying to rest, and not doing these things can almost feel like an act of self-expression, as you are showing the world that life is too hard and you want to give up. But it is essential that you do look after yourself, so you can regain your strength.

TASK FOR THE DAY

* Shower.
* Find your most favourite item of clothing and wear it.
* What do you love to eat? Cook it or buy it.
* What is your favourite movie? Watch it.
* What is your favourite book? Dig it out and reread it.
* Where is your favourite walk? Can you go there and breathe in fresh air?
* Who is your favourite person to chat with? Call them.
* Today is about you. Today is about acknowledging you matter.

Our lost children are not pain, they are not a wound, they are not the trauma – the loss is the agony, not the precious soul that was taken from us far too soon. So, when people say, 'Maybe you are best not to talk about them in case you reopen the wound' or 'Perhaps you are making it worse', they are simply not understanding that our children are the gift. They are the beautiful treasure people spend their life searching for. By talking about them, we heal. By sharing their story, however short it may have been, we cast a light in someone else's dark world. And, perhaps most importantly, we are acknowledging they were here, that their lives made a difference, that because they existed we are different – that, because of them, the world is a better place.

ZOË CLARK-COATES

DAY 3

I think many of us are taught to put pain into a nice neat parcel and hide it away, as we are encouraged by society to just put on a brave face and get on with life. While we do need to carry on with life – as sadly our bills still need to be paid, so we can keep a roof over our heads – we definitely should not be encouraged to run from pain. Sometimes we just need to yield to the agony, and immerse ourselves in our feelings and emotions so we can process them. Once they are processed and our brain has reluctantly come to terms with the trauma we have faced, the healing can commence.

TASK FOR THE DAY

What do you feel society is saying to you? Write down five messages you are hearing from those around you. Now consider if these are helpful. If they aren't helpful, consider how you should respond and move forwards.

1 _____

2 _____

3 _____

4 _____

5 _____

The day after my baby died, what shocked me the most was that the sun still rose, and the post still slipped through my mailbox, and I still got thirsty, and the birds still sang, and the traffic lights still changed colour . . . but my world had stopped, my planet had stopped spinning.

ZOË CLARK-COATES

DAY 4

We all have dreams and we all have a vision of how our life should look. Loss doesn't take these hopes and plans into account, it just rips them up in front of our eyes. I think one of the key parts of grief is accepting that in the briefest of moments life changed forever, that it no longer resembles what we had planned. This means processing the shock. Accepting the painful reality of life now being different, and then being willing to consider a new plan and a different future. None of this is easy, it is incredibly difficult, but once we have considered a new way forward it makes life feel a little more stable and back in control.

TASK FOR THE DAY

What three things would help you move forwards? Do you need to see a doctor and talk about your physical/emotional health? Do you need to change things at work? Do you need to join an exercise programme, so you feel fitter and stronger? Do you need to spend less time on social media, and more time enjoying nature?

1 _____

2 _____

3 _____

The mistake so many make when trying to help the bereaved is they tell those in mourning they should be thankful for having a heart that still beats in their chest. It is as though they feel that reminding them they have so much more life to live will encourage them to re-find their purpose. The truth is, this will never bring comfort to the broken-hearted; they feel no gratitude in being alive, they are just being made to feel guilty for wanting to die. So, if you want to help the grieving, don't tell them they should feel thankful, don't tell them they 'should' feel anything, just allow them to be, allow them to weep and allow them to crawl through the agony of loss – and, if you want to show love, get on your knees and silently crawl with them.

ZOË CLARK-COATES

DAY 5

Many associate the pain they are feeling with the loss they have experienced, and therefore fear letting go of the pain. They worry that if they don't experience the agony, they won't feel close to the person/child they have lost. Let me reassure you: your loved one isn't in the pain, they are in the love. The love that will never end. The love that will never dissipate. The love that will never be hidden. The pain can leave, the tears can go, and you will still be forever connected, by your endless, everlasting love.

TASK FOR THE DAY

Find a poem or a song that helps you express the love you feel.

It is okay to love them for ever. It is okay to speak their name. It is okay to miss them endlessly. It is okay to be confused. It is okay to be lost and fear never being found. It is okay to be scared of the darkness and long to see the light. It is okay to crave the old you while changing into the new you. It is okay to wish it was different and to dream of a happier ending.

This is the nature of grief, where everything is questioned. When you need reassurance that things are 'okay'. Where you long to be told you aren't going mad, you aren't 'abnormal'.

You just loved them more than words can ever say. Your heart just broke into so many pieces that breathing alone is an effort.

But grief is a fast-moving river, and as you grieve you are moving downstream. Let the current take you; you don't need to cling to the river bank. Even though you don't know how to swim, you will be okay.

ZOË CLARK-COATES

DAY 6

Friends can be such a great support when you are going through loss. Of course, there can be the odd person who isn't the greatest at emotional support, but there are also often unexpected treasures, people you never thought would show up in your moment of need who blow you away with their kindness. I always say grief is the ultimate life sieve – it reveals what matters and shows you people's true characters. While this sieve can unearth some potential issues, it can also make life so much richer for you in the future, so try to embrace it and not fear it.

TASK FOR THE DAY

Which of your friends have been your lifeline? Have any of your friends surprised you with their kindness and love?

Write down three things which have been true gifts to you, so you never forget them.

1 _____

2 _____

3 _____

Not a stillborn . . .
A precious child.

Not a miscarriage.
A son or daughter.

Not an ectopic pregnancy . . .
A little one that is adored.

Not a molar pregnancy . . .
A longed-for baby.

Forever missed.
Always loved.

* * * * * * * * * * * ZOË CLARK-COATES * * * * * * * * * *

DAY 7

So many people worry that they shouldn't talk of the baby they have lost. They fear people may think they aren't coping, or are dwelling in misery, or perhaps even seeking attention. Oh, how untrue these things are. Talking of the child you have lost does nothing more than show the world you have lost the one you adore. I know I say a lot throughout this book that talking is key, but that's only because it is so true, and people don't need to hear this only once, they need to hear it over and over again, so they feel encouraged to do it. So, let me encourage you to keep talking about your child, keep talking about the pain, keep talking about any feelings you encounter, so your heart and brain can start to heal.

TASK FOR THE DAY

Write down what you want the world to know about your child.

People need to be reminded that they can survive
the passage of grief. It is so easy to forget that when
fumbling around in the darkness of the pit. So let me be
the one to remind you today. You will make it through.
You will rediscover your joy. You will flourish again, and
you will do it to honour the one you have lost.

ZOË CLARK-COATES

DAY 8

How do you accept something that feels so utterly wrong? It is easy to accept things that have gone right, but how does something painful or crippling ever sit comfortably in your soul? I don't think it can, to be honest. Some things will never make sense, and will never, ever be okay – and that is what we have to come to terms with. It is only when life (or people) force us to try to be okay with what has happened that this internal fight occurs; the peace can only come when we accept that it doesn't make sense. That it is completely wrong. That the natural order of life has been broken, and we never need to be okay with that; we can just move forwards accepting that life is sometimes crap.

TASK FOR THE DAY

Take time out from thinking today, whether that be 15 minutes or 5 minutes. Free your mind from questions and expectations. Lie down, put on some music and just be. If thoughts pop into your mind, don't engage with them. Just focus on the music and let the bed or floor absorb your weight. This is your time to escape and give your brain a chance to rest.

Small things can trigger a fresh wave of grief – a
smell, a look or perhaps a song – and within seconds
you are flung into a time machine and are transported
back to that 'moment' when time stood still, and
the world had crashed at your feet.

ZOË CLARK-COATES

DAY 9

* *

When you lose a baby, you aren't just losing your child at x gestation, or at x years of age – you are losing them as a baby, as a toddler, as a seven-year-old, as a teenager, as an adult. This is why grief is a lifelong journey, as you will always be acutely aware of how old your child should be at every point in your life. While this can seem daunting early on in the grief journey, to even contemplate the walk of grief being so long, I can assure you it won't always feel like that. Once the acute pain subsides and the blackest part of grief fades, you just journey on with this awareness and it becomes part of who you are. I now love to remember each one of the babies I have lost. Thinking of them never makes me sad; I always remember them with a smile. People often assume grief is just about pain, but it isn't; it is also about expressing and carrying love.

TASK FOR THE DAY

What three things are you most sad about not knowing or seeing? For me, I wish I had known the colour of my children's eyes. I wish I had known what their personalities would have been like. I also wish I could have heard their laughs; you can tell a lot from a laugh, and as their mum I should know the sound of their laughter, as you should know the sound of your child's laugh.

1 _____

2 _____

3 _____

* *

When you survive loss, everyone is quick to tell
you how strong you are and how tough you must
be. But actually, no one has a choice to survive
grief, do they? It's not optional. You just have to
cry in the shower, sob into your pillow and
pray you will make it.

* * * * * * * * * * * ZOË CLARK-COATES * * * * * * * * * * *

DAY 10

When I hear people say they are fighting back the tears, my first question is always: why? Why would you want to fight away this beautiful expression of emotion? Tears have a voice, and that voice is so rarely listened to, but something magical happens if we do listen to what the tears are saying. Those droplets of water speak profound truth and tell life-changing stories. So, let me encourage you to weep whenever you need to. Sob on the floor. Howl in the shower. Fill your pillow with tears. Let your tears tell your story, and they will transport you to a place of healing.

TASK FOR THE DAY

Go to a private place where you fear no judgement and let the tears flow. Don't let that inner voice tell you not to go there just in case you can't stop once you have started; this will just keep you locked in the pain. Cry. Release the pain, which will in turn release the hormones and chemicals which tears of grief contain. Expect to feel drained following a release of powerful emotion, so ensure you have the time to recompose yourself, or a time to rest or even sleep.

I often used to say, 'I am fine, thank you' when people asked me how I was. Their response would just be to say, 'Great', and on we all moved. What I longed for them to say was, 'I know you aren't fine, but one day you will be.' To simply know my pain was acknowledged and my aching heart was being heard would have meant the world. This is the gift we can all give to anyone who is walking the path of grief. Listen to their whispers and breathe life into aching souls.

ZOË CLARK-COATES

DAY 11

I don't know if you are like me, but I fear looking weak, and worry that people may think I am not coping. I think it is odd that these worries ever even enter our mind, and maybe that's a society issue? Or perhaps it's due to how we were raised, if we have been conditioned to think of others before we consider what is actually best for our own well-being? Whatever the reason, there comes a time when we need to forget what others think, and be true to ourselves. When we fight conformity and embrace true self-expression, amazing things can happen – not only can we begin to heal, we also give others the freedom to be true to themselves.

TASK FOR THE DAY

Do you feel you act in a certain way due to societal pressure or because those around you have told you to conform? Do you feel you would be happier and more at peace if you acted differently from these expectations? If the answer is yes, consider how you can make changes. Going through significant loss blows your world to pieces, and at times you can make real changes as your life starts to be rebuilt. You don't need to put all the pieces back into the same place!

People told me I was brave not to give up, but want to know the truth? I did give up! We all give up! When the pain is all-consuming, when life has lost all meaning, we all scream at the sky, 'Enough!' But something magical happens when we quit; when we say, 'I can't take any more!' We discover life carries on regardless and, when we have nothing more to offer, a new strength is sent to carry us through.

ZOË CLARK-COATES

DAY 12

People often ask me when the missing them will end. The answer is simple: never! Sometimes this makes me feel like the bearer of bad news, but it is actually a gift. Why would anyone want the missing them to end? If you didn't miss them, it would mean you were glad they had left, and of course you would never feel like that. So why is missing them a gift? Well, for me, the missing them shows the world and myself that I loved them endlessly. It shows that they left a space in my life that can never and should never be filled by anyone, as only they can fit that exact space. It also shows one other important thing – it shows that they mattered then, they matter now and they will always matter.

TASK FOR THE DAY

Try to rewire your thinking. The world tells us that missing people is wrong, and we need to move on and get over it. It tells us that missing someone is a curse rather than a blessing. While we feel a need to fight our natural feelings (which is to miss someone for ever), we resent having these feelings present in our life, and this can become a source of conflict in our minds. If we can change our thinking and accept it's a gift and a blessing to miss someone, we can find room for these feelings in our life, and naturally adjust to them. Once we accept it's normal and right to feel this way, we also leave no room for feelings of shame and guilt. I promise you that if you can untangle what you have been taught and accept this new way of thinking, it will be life-changing.

* *

Some may ask why I speak of the children I have lost, but that to me is like asking me why I talk about my husband, or of the children that are with me. My babies are not a dirty secret, they are not something to be ashamed of. They are part of me, and I am part of them. I may not have the privilege of raising them, but I do have the honour of remembering them and speaking of the beautiful impact they have had on my life.

* * * * * * * * * * * * ZOË CLARK-COATES * * * * * * * * * * * *

DAY 13

* *

Chaos.

Grief and loss bring chaos. It is like our lives are put into a washing machine and all hell breaks loose when it's whizzing around in circles. Everything in that machine changes shape. Dye leaks out of items and runs into other items. Things that should only be handwashed have also been put in there, and are then destroyed. But what also happens is that some things come out better than before. Some items come out clean and fresh. Some items come out a different shape, but that turns out to be a better fit than before. So while the washing machine is a harrowing experience, it can reap good things too. So why do I share this? Not because I want you to look on the bright side – as there is *no* bright side when it comes to death and loss – but because I want you to know there is hope post-loss, that good things can be birthed from tragedy, as I needed to hear this when I was in the depths of loss. I needed someone to be a lighthouse in the darkness, to show me life could be better down the line and some of the pain I was experiencing could be turned into purpose. So try not to give up hope – hold on. The washing machine will eventually stop.

TASK FOR THE DAY

Is there anything you would like to be different post-loss? Would you like to change jobs? Would you like to find new friends? Would you like to take up a different hobby? Would you like to look more at the meaning of life? Use the pain from loss to help transform your life into something better.

It's okay to be different.

It's okay to be bruised.

It is okay to show one's scars . . .

I don't know when the world started to tell us perfection was beautiful, but it is wrong. The truth is, vulnerability is breathtaking. Being authentic is inspiring and walking with our head held high, carrying no shame from our journey, is where real beauty can be found.

ZOË CLARK-COATES

DAY 14

What happens if you can't cry? What happens if the tears just won't flow?

Firstly, don't panic. Sometimes the shock of loss prevents tears from being able to come. A lack of tears does not mean you don't love the one you have lost, and it certainly doesn't mean you didn't care. Everyone is different, and for some their natural response may not be to weep on the floor; it may be to write a song, or run a marathon. Grief can be expressed in so many different ways and what I hope you have learnt from this book is that grief is as personal as your fingerprint. So, the only important thing is finding your way to express your grief so that it can be channelled and processed.

TASK FOR THE DAY

Can you think of different ways you can express your grief?
Write a list of ways you could express the pain you are
feeling, which would help you move through the grieving
process.

1 _____

2 _____

3 _____

4 _____

* *

The thing with grief is it can catch you when you
least expect it. Maybe that's in a shop where you see
an item of clothing that your loved one would have
cherished. Maybe it's at the park when you see a new
mother pushing along her baby in a sparkling new
pram. Perhaps it's when you are lying in bed at night
and the pillow next to you is missing your soulmate's
dent. Whenever and wherever it catches you,
it's gut-wrenching and has the power to leave
you speechless.

ZOË CLARK-COATES

DAY 15

Past trauma – Remember I previously mentioned that grief is the ultimate life sieve? This really comes into effect when a person has been through previous life traumas or upsets, as grief can bring any unresolved pain or issues to the surface. There really couldn't be a worse time to have to deal with these old emotional scars: when you are grieving, the grief alone is utterly overwhelming without having to deal with old life issues as well, but sadly we often have no control over them re-surfacing. You have two options if/when this happens: 1. You can find a way to shove these emotions back into the box from which they emerged (which is tricky, but is sometimes possible); 2. You use this time to deal with the unhealed wounds. Yes, the timing is rubbish, but by dealing with them you are giving yourself the best chance possible of a happier life. If you feel flooded and overwhelmed, I would strongly recommend seeking external help from a professional therapist, who can help you untangle the turmoil. Use this time of grieving to heal and resist the urge to put a cork in the bottle and throw it out to sea.

TASK FOR THE DAY

Has grief brought past upset to the surface for you? If it has, consider how you could/should deal with it. Do you need professional help? Or do you just need to sit and talk with a family member or friend? A helpful exercise can be to write down all the things that have emerged while you are grieving and see if there is a common thread to them all.

Grief is sacred; it is liquid love streaming from
the cracks of a broken heart.

ZOË CLARK-COATES

DAY 16

C. S. Lewis said that he never knew grief felt so like fear, and it is so true. I think grief does feel like fear, but I also think that, when grief consumes you, fear also uses the same door and enters our life. Fear of the future. Fear of what may happen next. Fear of feeling out of control. Fear of the unknown. Fear of more loss. Fear of looking weak. Fear of medical intervention. Fear of how people may react around us. The list goes on and on, as there are a million worries many of us will experience. So how do we cope with the fear? Firstly, I think knowing we are not alone in experiencing this paralysing fear helps greatly, as fear can make us feel isolated and like we are the only one in the world feeling it. I also think that knowing it's common for most people to experience this stops people feeling like they are going crazy. We do have to be careful not to give fear too much space in our minds, however, and also not to give in to the fear. For example, the fear may tell you never to go out just in case you end up crying in public. But a good response to this would be to do the exact thing fear is telling you not to do – go out and if you cry, you cry! Fear will want to lock you into a dark and private cell, so refuse to be trapped by it. Let the inner lion within you roar, and, believe me, fear will eventually flee.

TASK FOR THE DAY

What have you become scared of? How can you fight the fear?

1 _____

★ I can fight it by

┌───┐
│   │
│   │
└───┘

2 _____

★ I can fight it by

┌───┐
│   │
│   │
└───┘

* *

There was a time when I was consumed by fear.

The enemy seemed large and terrifying.

Then I started to develop tenacity and resilience,
and that warrior spirit that had become hidden in
me during the battle rose up once again.

This was a life-changing experience, my 'Wonder
Woman' moment.

I discovered I had more faith than fear, more hope than
doubt. And though I felt weak I was in fact badass.

ZOË CLARK-COATES

DAY 17

When people ask me to explain what baby loss is like, the first analogy that leaps to my mind is this. Imagine you are holding on to your child's hand over a cliff edge. You are using every bit of strength to hold on to them, but then they let go. You watch them plummet to their death. Everything within you screams 'No!' as you watch them falling. You scream that you never let go, you would have never, ever let go, even if you had died in the process. This wasn't your choice; this wasn't something you could control. Baby loss is torture. Recurrent loss is prolonged torture. It is hard to explain, this type of loss, to someone who has never experienced it, but sometimes it's asked of those who have gone through it to explain, so others who haven't can gain insight.

TASK FOR THE DAY

How would you explain loss? Write down how you explain loss to someone. Sometimes verbalising our pain helps.

* *

What can you do if you don't want to live without someone who has gone? How do you simply survive the pain, the heartbreak, and find your will to continue? Well, you admit how you are feeling. You scream, you shout, you weep on your bedroom floor and you hold on to the edge of that mountain cliff, until your desire to live outweighs your hope to die.

ZOË CLARK-COATES

DAY 18

Once a parent, always a parent.

Once you have conceived a child, you are a parent; whether you have empty arms or full arms, it makes no difference to this hard-earned title. Once you see those two lines on a pregnancy test stick, a door opens – a beautiful door, and this door can never be closed once it's opened. At times, post-loss, I wished this wasn't the case. I wished I could go back to being just me, as the pain of having no child to raise but feeling like a mum (because I was one) was agonising. I also felt like I had to constantly defend my right to be called a mum, and I know so many parents feel like this when their child has gone before them. So why do I share this? Well, I think it is important for you to hear that I acknowledge you are a parent, now and for ever. It's not just you declaring it; I declare it with you.

TASK FOR THE DAY

How have you changed, now that you are a parent?

* *

Initially, the pain was all-consuming. It was like the raw
agony had sucked every bit of breath from my lungs.
But after some time the intensity subsided. Was that
because the grief was reducing or was it simply
because I had become accustomed to living with
the weight of the loss? Who knows! But being able
to take those shallow breaths again gave me enough
oxygen to sustain me to the next day.

* * * * * * * * * * ZOË CLARK-COATES * * * * * * * * * *

DAY 19

How can a person feel this much pain? A question I would often ask myself, especially in the dark hours of the night when I felt scared due to the volume of pain I was experiencing. The pain felt like a giant before me, and the thought of continuing forwards with this pain hovering over me was beyond daunting. I simply didn't understand how the pain could be so great and so consuming, and then I had a lightbulb moment – the pain was this huge and unending because my love for my child was unlimited. With unlimited love comes unlimited pain if the person is lost. This realisation stopped me questioning it, and I accepted it for what it was, and when I stopped fighting the pain, it became less scary. It stopped being an enemy and became an often-silent companion, until it was time for it to leave my life and only the love for my child remained.

TASK FOR THE DAY

Try to write a poem or quote about the pain you are feeling. If you allow yourself to express your pain creatively, it can help transform it.

* *

We all have a view of what 'broken' looks like, and I think because of this we can assume people who are broken-hearted are fine if they are smiling.

Please know that grief-stricken people still smile, they still chat, still engage, still work, still party, still talk . . . because they have to.

* * * * * * * * * ZOË CLARK-COATES * * * * * * * * * *

DAY 20

* *

Can we prepare for loss? No, I don't think we can. We can certainly start grieving before the loss happens, but that is very different from actually preparing for the trap door to open, just in case it does open. If we try to prepare, we just rob ourselves of experiencing true joy in the moment. So often people say to me, 'If only I hadn't celebrated the fact I was pregnant, then it wouldn't hurt as much now.' While it is natural to feel like this, it is not accurate, as the pain of loss is just as huge whether you celebrated or not; but one way you experienced the happiness and excitement, and the other way you just felt the pain and grief. Your brain may try to encourage you to be more pessimistic in future, and to expect a life of tragedy, as a form of self-protection. I am a strong believer that this helps no one, and just means you are then faced with a life of less hope, of less peace and of less joy. I think it is a lot better to hold on to hope with both hands. To celebrate every ounce of happiness that lands in your lap, and to remain as positive as possible about the future. If you sadly need to face loss again, you deal with it then, but at least you have had seasons of glorious joy.

TASK FOR THE DAY

Have you become pessimistic about life? Write down two areas where your thoughts have centred on the negative, and then write down how you feel you could overcome that thinking.

1 _____

* I can overcome this thinking by

_____

_____

_____

2 _____

* I can overcome this thinking by

_____

_____

_____

* *

It shocks me how everyone assumes they know how
another should grieve. 'They should do it this way.'
'They are doing it wrong!' 'Why are they still weeping?'
So many questions, expectations and conflicting
opinions. There is only one truth, and that is this:

They are grieving their way and that is the
'only' right way.

* * * * * * * * * * ZOË CLARK-COATES * * * * * * * * * * *

DAY 21

People used to tell me I was brave not to give up, but do you want to know the truth? I did; a hundred times a day, thousands of times a week, I gave up. I screamed, I yelled and sobbed, saying, 'That's it, I am done.' The pain overwhelmed me and I was fed up with being broken, down on my knees. So if you are kicking yourself for giving up, please know this: *everyone* gives up. When the pain is all-consuming and life has lost its meaning, we all scream at the sky and shout, 'I can't take any more!' In that moment, we discover that life carries on regardless of whether we have the strength to continue or not, and all we need to do is sit for a while and wait for a fresh wave of courage to be bestowed upon us to refuel us for the next part of the journey.

TASK FOR THE DAY

There is something extremely cathartic in screaming at the sky, in shouting and releasing that internal pain. If you can find a place where you can go to scream, holler, wail and release some of the pain, do it today. You may also want to go to the gym and put on a pair of boxing gloves and hit a punch bag. Physical acts can truly help emotional pain.

* *

When you have run out of tears and you are just left feeling empty and broken, this is when you need to search for the light. Even a fragment of sunshine will enable you to find those pieces of your broken heart lying on the floor. Slowly gather them, and your journey of healing will have begun.

* * * * * * * * * * ZOË CLARK-COATES * * * * * * * * * *

DAY 22

People often say, 'You will conquer this grief', as if it's an obstacle course you have to pole-vault over. But no one conquers grief, it is something you have to face, not fight; it can't be skipped over and it can't be defeated. You have to allow it to surround you like fog on a mountain top, and only when the fog rises can you see the path in front of you. It is not the enemy, even though it often feels like it. It is most certainly a giant – but it's a giant made out of love, pain, lessons, gentleness and a million other emotions. If we welcome the giant around the table, and don't try to make it stay on the other side of the door, it can teach us so much about ourselves and the world.

TASK FOR THE DAY

How would you describe grief? What does this giant look like in your life?

I expected to miss you in those silent solitary moments
and I knew it would haunt me through the dark hours
of the night. What I didn't expect was that the pain
would have the ability to knock me off my feet while
I was at a party, when I was laughing with friends,
when I was enjoying a meal with family. Nothing
prepares you for the power of grief.

ZOË CLARK-COATES

DAY 23

Who looked into your eyes and whispered in your ear that you are not enough? Who told you that you were responsible for this pain? Was it a family member? Was it a friend? Was it society? Or perhaps it was yourself? Whoever it was, they were not telling you the truth.

* You are enough.
* You are not responsible for this pain.
* You are worthy of love.
* You deserve to be praised and cared for.
* You do not need to keep your wounds hidden any longer, my friend.

Bravely show them to the world and let them heal.

TASK FOR THE DAY

Write a letter to yourself, telling yourself why you are strong, and why you are proud of yourself. You can empower yourself to move forwards. Be your own cheerleader.

Dear Me,

There are a million things I want to tell you, but the most important of all is: 'I will always love you.'

ZOË CLARK-COATES

DAY 24

Society often tells us that if something is common, we should accept it and not be overly bothered by it. People often used to remind me how common miscarriage is, as if that would make me feel better. While it was nice to know I wasn't the only person in the world going through baby loss, knowing it happened in one in four pregnancies didn't make my pain any less; it just made me acutely aware of how many broken-hearted people were walking on this planet.

It is strange how people like to minimise pain, but I want to assure you that even if those around you don't acknowledge the gravity of your loss, I do. I know you are broken right now. I know no words I can offer will take that pain away from you. But sometimes it is enough to know our pain has been seen, and our loss has been recognised.

TASK FOR THE DAY

I want you to fill this box with all the words you feel right now. Write them simply, or write them in different sizes and different colours.

* *

I had seen others journey through loss, I had read the books, I thought I understood it. But all the knowledge in the world, and all the preparation one can ever do, won't ever prepare you for how losing a loved one feels. I had heard the word 'broken' used, and I couldn't quite understand what that meant . . . until I broke. It is when the world seems black, devoid of hope, and you pray the world stops spinning so you can get off. All-consuming pain with no respite. That is what it means to be broken.

* * * * * * * * * * ZOË CLARK-COATES * * * * * * * * * *

DAY 25

'What do you need?' I was asked this so many times when walking through grief. I often had no clue what I needed; my mind was overwhelmed and flooded with emotion. Sometimes I felt utterly numb, at other times a million different emotions consumed me. There were many occasions when I couldn't have conducted a conversation, but I still wanted to be with people, as I felt so lost and scared by the feelings I was trying to process. At those times I was only capable of sitting and staring at the wall, and I just needed someone to sit and stare at the wall with me. I wish I had been able to tell people that.

TASK FOR THE DAY

Think about what you need. If you can't find the words in the moment, perhaps take some time to write it down, and then give it to your friends and family to read. It can be incredibly hard to support someone through grief, and just giving people some pointers can be a huge help to them, but also to yourself down the line.

* *

You love me beyond my brokenness and cover me
with compassion beyond my comprehension. Instead
of telling me to not cry, you sat beside me and
collected each tear that fell from my eyes.
You . . . yes, you . . . made me feel truly loved.

* * * * * * * * * * ZOË CLARK-COATES * * * * * * * * * *

DAY 26

What is your most difficult time each day? Mine was definitely the silent hours between 1am and 6am. These were the hours when grief consumed me and drained the room of all oxygen. When it became hard to breathe and surviving the loss seemed incomprehensible. Daylight seemed elusive and the birds were not even tempted to sing. I would often doubt that I could survive those nights, but I did, and you too will survive your haunting hours. Hold on, my friend. The sun will rise and hope will return.

TASK FOR THE DAY

Take 15 minutes to do something just for you. Whether it be reading a book, soaking in the bath, enjoying a coffee while looking at your garden – whatever you choose to do today, these minutes are your minutes and I hope they bring a smile to your face.

To be told my baby had died was incomprehensible. To continue living when my world was lying shattered at my feet was unthinkable. But I survived it and I promise you, my friend, you will survive it too.

ZOË CLARK-COATES

DAY 27

From the moment I discovered I was pregnant, I was constantly thinking of the baby I was carrying. From the moment I discovered my baby had died, I was constantly thinking of the child I had lost. Oh, how I wished there was some sort of magic switch that I could have flicked off so the endless thoughts, the emotion and the feelings would just vanish. I never found the switch and I guess you haven't found it either, so the only option is to live with the thoughts. What I can assure you of is this: although the thoughts are initially all-consuming, they do get less and less, until one day they no longer haunt you. Time is the only thing that helps, as it takes weeks (and perhaps even months) for the brain to adjust to this new reality. So hold on; it gets easier.

TASK FOR THE DAY

What are the thoughts that haunt you? Write them down.
Once these emotions are expressed or verbalised, they can
at times dissipate, as they are just seeking to be heard.

Countless babies are lost before birth, during birth, post
birth or in early years.

That does not make it okay.

It does not mean people should expect it.

It definitely doesn't mean people should or
can prepare for it.

It just means a lot of people have a piece
of their heart missing.

ZOË CLARK-COATES

DAY 28

Grief has so many layers. After losing a baby, it is obvious that a person will be grieving the child they have lost, but it may surprise you that they could also be grieving over many other things simultaneously. When I lost my babies, I grieved being pregnant. I loved growing a person; yes, I hated the pregnancy symptoms, but I loved my baby bump and loved feeling my babies grow, turn and kick. When my pregnancies abruptly stopped, I was devastated to no longer be pregnant.

I also grieved losing my joy. One day I was beyond happy, the next day I was beyond crushed, and I couldn't even imagine a time I would smile again. I grieved for the fact I no longer cared about normal everyday things. Loss made these simple things feel irrelevant, even though they had previously brought me such joy.

These are just a few of the things I grieved.

TASK FOR THE DAY

What are you grieving for besides the loss of your child?

1 _____

2 _____

3 _____

4 _____

* *

Be patient.

Give yourself time to heal.

Rebuilding yourself following heartbreak
is a slow process and it is something
that can't be rushed.

So stop. Breathe. Wait.

* * * * * * * * * * ZOË CLARK-COATES * * * * * * * * * *

DAY 29

The silent scream. Only those who have ever produced this soul-churning scream will know what it is. When you fall to your knees and a silent scream leaves your lips, but there is no sound at all to be heard in this earthly realm. (I do wonder if it can perhaps be heard in another place? Perhaps Heaven?) For me, the scream stopped once the shock passed; for others, I know the silent scream is ongoing and they believe it will never stop. One thing I can promise you is this: if your scream remains, you will learn to navigate around it, and in time you will get used to that holler humming in the background.

TASK FOR THE DAY

What would you tell someone who had just lost a loved
one? What advice would you give them?

* *

I didn't think I could survive pain like that. Before
experiencing the heartache, I presumed I would crumble.
While journeying it, I thought I might die from grief. In
the weeks that followed, I assumed I would be broken for
ever. So I learnt a valuable lesson – I can and did survive
the unimaginable and you will too.

* * * * * * * * * * ZOË CLARK-COATES * * * * * * * * * *

DAY 30

People kept asking me if I was ready. Ready to move forwards. Ready to try again for another child. How does one ever feel ready? What does feeling ready even mean? Does it mean we feel brave? Does it mean we feel sure and confident? If that is the case, I rarely feel ready for anything. What I have learnt on my journey is this: waiting to feel ready stops people from achieving their life goals. We just have to step forwards terrified. Heart racing. Hands shaking. Lip quivering. Stomach churning. And once we reach our end goal we can finally see – feeling ready is simply a myth.

TASK FOR THE DAY

What have you been postponing until you feel ready? Do you think you could take a chance and just move forwards? Now may not be the right time, of course, but perhaps it is? Maybe you just need to bravely step out of your comfort zone.

You were hidden from the world when you grew in the secret place. But now I tell the world of your existence, for you, little one, are connected to my soul.

ZOË CLARK-COATES

DAY 31

* *

I was so blessed to have my soulmate Andy by my side through loss, but so many people have to grieve with little or no support. If you can't share the pain and emotions you are experiencing with someone who empathises, you can quickly feel lost and isolated. I wanted everyone around me to comprehend that my world had stopped spinning . . . this is how I felt:

> *You died but still . . . the dawn breaks. The seas roar. The birds soar. The butterflies dance. The lightning strikes. The stars shine. The seasons fade. The earth spins. The icecaps thaw. The sun sets. But . . . my heart breaks. My soul cries. My eyes weep. My arms ache. My joy sleeps.*

But how does one communicate this? And perhaps more importantly, how can we ensure those around us understand this? One way is by writing down how we feel, perhaps in letter form so we can carefully articulate the journey of loss.

TASK FOR THE DAY

Write your own letter to a loved one or a friend. Think of the things you want to say, that you may never have thought to express.

* *

I want to tell every person in the whole world about you. I want the moon to know how I love you. The stars to know how I adore you. The sun to know how I will always miss you.

* * * * * * * * * * ZOË CLARK-COATES * * * * * * * * * *

DAY 32

It is common to fear being defined by the circumstances one has lived through, and if this becomes an overwhelming worry it is easy to change the dialogue used. I want to encourage you to stick with the fearless truth of your story, and not to worry about how society may see you. Don't get me wrong – I was concerned about this too, but along the way I learnt that most people don't look at those who talk of their pain and vulnerabilities through pity spectacles; they look at people with respect. When we open up our hearts and souls to the world, people want to come closer, they don't run in the opposite direction (well, authentic folk don't). People crave honesty, they long to see individuals displaying true sincerity, so please don't let fear rob you of speaking your authentic truth.

TASK FOR THE DAY

Write down exactly how you feel today, then pluck up the courage to tell someone what you have written.

When . . .

When . . . you find it hard to remember the last time you looked forward to something.

When . . . you don't remember a time when you weren't consumed with pain.

This is the time 'when' you need to hold on.

When . . . you need to trust life will get easier.

When . . . you need to believe broken hearts can heal.

When . . . you need to trust that tomorrow could possibly be 'when'.

ZOË CLARK-COATES

DAY 33

* *

I think most people who go through loss will tell you that when people around you are complaining about having sleepless nights with their babies, or moaning about stretch marks, it kind of grates. It is hard to hear anyone complaining about something you would give anything to have. The temptation when you hear someone saying, 'Wow, I had a tough night, the baby cried for hours' is to yell, 'Do you know what I would give to be kept up all night by a baby?!' Of course, I wouldn't encourage you to say this to anyone, but I wanted to include it here to show you that you aren't alone if you are feeling this right now. While we often need to hold our tongues in these moments, resentment/irritation can sneakily creep up on us. The best way to process these feelings is to talk about them with a safe person (i.e. someone who would not report it back to the person saying it), as just by verbalising the frustration it can help diminish or eliminate the feelings you are experiencing.

TASK FOR THE DAY

Write a list of the things you are struggling to hear and deal with. Once you have written the list, consider how you could respond in a kind way, to change the future dialogue.

I can always recognise those who have been broken.
For they now carry a light – a light that can only be
bestowed on those who have been shattered
by heartbreak.

They are filled with greater levels of compassion,
of empathy and of kindness, for they know
first-hand what true pain feels like.

ZOË CLARK-COATES

DAY 34

Anniversaries and occasions.

For some, these are dates to look forward to, as those around them join them in talking about the baby they have lost; for others, the days bring a fresh wave of grief and can make the feelings of isolation seem suffocating. Others don't mark any dates in the diary and the days pass without notice. I fall into this last category: I chose not to carve out any dates in my calendar; perhaps that's because I have had repeated loss, and there would be too many dates to circle, but it could also be because I made a conscious choice to celebrate and talk about my babies 365 days a year, and that meant I didn't feel a need to have set days each year to process pain or celebrate my children. However, for some these dates will forever be ingrained and they have no choice but to acknowledge them in their lives. So, what do I suggest to people to help them get through birth or death anniversaries, due dates, loss dates, etc.? I always recommend they find something they love to do to mark these dates. Perhaps that's a walk in the park, maybe it's planting a new plant or tree, maybe it's going to a lovely café and having a slice of their favourite cake – but do something that makes you smile, as that means you can remember your little one with a smile. Don't get me wrong – you may need to weep a river on those days and that's okay; it's a grief layer being processed. But if you can also do something you enjoy, it can help with the agony of the day.

TASK FOR THE DAY

What do you love to do? Can you think of something you could do yearly to celebrate your little one if you do want to mark the dates on your calendar?
  Write your ideas here:

Talk about it. Then talk some more. Then a little more.

The story you hold deep in your heart wants
to be told – needs to be told.

It is in the telling.

It is in the sharing.

It is in the revealing of your soul that the healing begins.

ZOË CLARK-COATES

DAY 35

It is very common post-loss to feel you are spending your life apologising for things that just flew out of your mouth. Grief seems to remove a filter, and without even meaning to be rude you may have found yourself saying the most awful things to the people around you. People often say to me 'Maybe it would be easier if I walked around with a sign saying "I am sorry", as I seem to offend people without even trying.' So if you feel this, know you are not alone. When you are trying to process pain and deal with profound loss, it is very difficult to control your emotions and your tongue, and one of the horrible side effects of this, is sadly putting your foot in it on a regular basis. So just be honest, be willing to apologise, and ask for grace from the people who love you.

TASK FOR THE DAY

Tell your story here (if you need more space, write your story elsewhere and use this space for thoughts):

* *

If today you are hurting. If tomorrow you are weeping.
That is okay. My friend, your heart is just healing.

* * * * * * * * * * * * ZOË CLARK-COATES * * * * * * * * * * * *

DAY 36

Loss divides your life into before and after.

Nothing looks or feels the same post-loss. Why is this? I believe it is because you change as a person so radically once you have lost a child that the world seems very different. It's like you have stepped through a door you never knew was there, and that door was firmly locked behind you as you went through it. There is no return to the old you, or that past world, and this is why life divides into before and after. While this can be traumatising and something in itself to grieve for, it can also be liberating. You now have the chance to recreate how you want the world to look. It's a blank piece of paper. Yes, it may be soggy with tears for some time, but it's still blank. Maybe it's time to make new friends? Maybe it's time to consider a change of direction with your career? Perhaps it's time to start a new hobby? When I made these changes in my life, they felt like gifts from my babies, like they were gifting me additional levels of happiness. Loss doesn't need only to bring heartbreak; your baby can also bring you beautiful, life-changing gifts.

TASK FOR THE DAY

Consider what gifts your babies have brought or could still bring you to make your life better:

1 _____

2 _____

3 _____

4 _____

5 _____

* *

Where does hope rest? I guess it's different in every person, but everyone can find their source. Search for that place in your soul where happiness once sat comfortably next to peace. Where your sense of purpose drove you forwards, and fear couldn't even stop you facing giants. In that secret place is your reserve of hope, and once it's rediscovered a journey can begin.

* * * * * * * * * * ZOË CLARK-COATES * * * * * * * * * * *

DAY 37

There is no hierarchy in grief.

The world often tells us that loss past x point is worse than at y point. Or a child you lose at x age is worse than losing a child aged y. I find this extraordinarily hard to understand and refuse to accept it, and will spend my life fighting this utterly wrong belief. Loss is loss. Grief is grief. Someone's age doesn't denote their worth, their place in this world or the significance of them as a person. If you lost a baby at six weeks, at 40 weeks, four weeks post-birth or at any point, you have the right to grieve. No one has the right to diminish your grief or your pain, or tell you how your loss was less important or notable than another's loss. There is simply no hierarchy in grief and, if we can collectively use our voices to say this, I think we will become a better, more compassionate society, one that supports without prejudice anyone who is hurting.

TASK FOR THE DAY

Use this space to write down the misconceptions you feel surround your loss. Perhaps people have presumed that due to your early pregnancy gestation the birth of your child was easy, as the word 'miscarriage' is so often used without people realising it means you delivered your baby? Perhaps you had a stillbirth – do people think there was no beauty in the birth, only pain?

Your time on earth was brief, and the chapter detailing
your existence seems so small in the story of my life.
But you were the plot changer. The colour giver. The
character builder. The joy bringer. Once you were
created, no page was ever the same again

ZOË CLARK-COATES

DAY 38

✳ ✳

Good and bad care post-loss.

How you are treated when you are going through loss makes the world of difference in how you process the pain and trauma attached to loss. If you received poor care, I can only say how sorry I am, as everyone should be treated with true compassion when journeying through one of the most traumatic life events. If you received excellent care, I am so pleased, and I know you will be able to speak of how empathy and kindness made your experience so much easier.

So, what do we do if we didn't get good care? We speak about it. We write to the GP, hospital, or to whoever fell below our expected standard. Now, I know this is easy to say but hard to do, however it's only when we speak out and hold people to account that things change. And, yes, I know it won't bring your baby back, and it may feel pointless in the scheme of things; but it isn't pointless, it will make a difference, so please take 20 minutes to write about your experience.

What do you do if you had great care? Speak about it and also write to the people who provided that care. When we take the time to offer praise and gratitude to care-givers, it makes them feel appreciated, but just as importantly it encourages good practice. So please thank and praise all who cared for you well.

TASK FOR THE DAY

Write to your care-givers and tell them about your great, or poor, care. Tell them about the treatment you received and how it made you feel.

* *

Sometimes people just need time.

Time to sit.

Time to just 'be' with the pain.

Time to let the tears pool.

Time to let the heart mend.

Time to accept life will never be the same again.

The issue for many?

They are rarely given 'time'.

* * * * * * * * * * ZOË CLARK-COATES * * * * * * * * * *

DAY 39

What do you do when you can't face another day, when the pain is too overwhelming? You have two choices: you can either try to run from it, which I can tell you now is pretty hard to do, and nine times out of 10 it will chase after you and will eventually catch you when you least expect it; or you yield to the pain. You dive in; you lie on the floor and let the pain surround you. You don't fight the tears, you let those body-shaking sobs consume your soul. You throw down your armour and say, 'I will no longer battle with these emotions, I surrender.'

When we surrender, we let grief take us to the next level. The tears transport us to somewhere new. It takes real courage to face pain like this head-on, so believe me when I say I am not trying to make this sound simple and easy. It's heartbreaking and possibly one of the toughest things one can do in this life – but by doing it you will be helping yourself in the long term.

TASK FOR THE DAY

Are you ready to take off your armour and lay down your sword? Will you just look pain in the eye and say, 'I will not run from you. I will simply let it flow through me and transform me as it runs through my veins.' If you are ready to do this, try this exercise:

Lie on the floor and clench every muscle in your body.

Screw up your face into a grimace and squeeze your hands into tight fists. Think of the emotional pain you are carrying. Hold for five seconds and then release fully. As you release, imagine yourself removing the armour you have been wearing and let the tears flow.

I find it helps to play music loudly when doing this. My song of choice is 'Hallelujah' by Jeff Buckley.

Please know that this exercise can be exhausting emotionally, so don't do it just before leaving for work or an event. Take a few hours afterwards to regroup and to relax.

* *

Baby loss =

A million 'what-if's.

A billion 'if-only's.

A trillion 'I-wish's.

ZOË CLARK-COATES

DAY 40

How often have we been told not to cry, or perhaps how many times have we told others not to cry? Society doesn't allow much space for weeping; we have been taught wrongly that to be strong means showing no or very little emotion. Yes, of course we can accept the odd pretty tear falling down a person's cheek, and may even be touched at seeing it before us, but it's different if someone is sobbing hysterically at our feet. If we are the one weeping, it feels messy, ugly and out of control. If we are the ones witnessing it, it can make us feel helpless and inept at dealing with such visible distress. But this is where we have gone wrong as humans. Emotion, *all* emotion is what makes us human; we should welcome the heart-wrenching sobs as much as we welcome the belly-doubling hysterical laughs. Life is amazing, but it can also be utterly crap. It can be beautiful and so very ugly. It can bring unending joy and endless pain. But we survive it by embracing every moment, by allowing ourselves and others to express it all – whether that be by weeping an ocean of tears, or by laughing till tears of joy roll down our cheeks.

TASK FOR THE DAY

Let the tears roll. Tears of grief and sadness are made of a different substance from tears of joy – how amazing is that? They contain hormones and chemicals, and it is essential we let them out so they can't cause damage to us emotionally and/or physically. So be kind to yourself and let them flow today. It may help to put on a piece of music, or go into the shower . . .

* *

You have so much more life to experience.

More love. More pain.

More joy. More suffering.

Grasp everything with two hands.

Feel it all.

It is only when we embrace both the dark and the light that we can live an extraordinary life.

* * * * * * * * * * *   ZOË CLARK-COATES   * * * * * * * * * * *

DAY 41

How can you let go of someone or something you have wanted so much? I wish there was a skill to make this easier, but sadly there isn't. It will never be easy letting go of a person you have loved dearly, but equally I don't think it should be easy. It should be gut-wrenching, it should be a battle, it should tear our hearts apart. Loss should be incomprehensible and bring us to our knees. That pain shows the love. Those tears reveal the heartbreak. And while we have to let go physically of the person, they will never leave our hearts, our minds, our lives. All those we have loved and lost remain on the pages of our books for ever.

TASK FOR THE DAY

Saying goodbye to a person's physical body is so incredibly hard. Maybe for you that will take place at a funeral; perhaps it is alone in your bathroom if you have had a very early miscarriage. Wherever and whenever it is, it will be a moment that lives with you for ever. To come to terms with that process, I want to encourage you to talk about the event. By talking about it, you allow your brain to accept what has happened and eventually, over time, you may feel more at peace.

As I resurfaced from the blackest part of grief, I quickly learnt I should stop seeking the big moments. You know, those moments you crave with the same desperation as a person crawling in the desert seeking water. Moments that feel so elusive and unreachable, like . . .

* Feeling total peace in your soul.

* Feeling excited about the year ahead.

* Not being consumed with pain.

* Not fearing tears could spontaneously spring from your eyes.

Instead, I needed to look towards the little moments . . .

* The smile that broke forth without any warning when something amused me.

* The kindness of a stranger who asked me how I was.

* The taste of that sweet peach that was nurtured and grown for me to enjoy.

* The joy I felt seeing my friend get their wish granted.

And this is how my journey changed. I learnt that life could be all kinds of wonderful just by appreciating the little moments.

ZOË CLARK-COATES

DAY 42

✳ ✳

Feeling guilt over grieving.

Often people message me saying they feel guilty grieving as their baby was a young gestation, or perhaps they lost following IVF and never got a positive pregnancy test result. Whatever the reason for the guilt they carry, I always say the same. Your grief is valid and it is okay to grieve for your baby, it is okay to grieve for the space you had held for a baby to fill, it's okay to grieve for the baby you longed to have but never got to conceive. It's okay! Let go of any guilt you put on your own shoulders, and disregard any guilt others placed in your hands to carry. You have full permission to grieve.

TASK FOR THE DAY

Are you carrying guilt? List the things you feel guilty about, and then decide how you can lay down that guilt and walk into freedom.

1 _____

2 _____

3 _____

There will be days where you are hit by a fresh wave of grief and you will doubt how far you have swum in the ocean of mourning. Let me reassure you that these waves are part of the journey, they won't put you back. In fact, they do the exact opposite; they carry you forwards if you don't fight them – just hold on to your life belt and let the current carry you on. You won't drown, but you may need to tell yourself this a hundred times a day. Let it become your mantra: 'I won't drown; I am just learning to swim.'

ZOË CLARK-COATES

DAY 43

Wanting to protect others.

It is so normal to want to protect those around us from the pain we ourselves are walking, so if you are feeling this, please know you are not alone. I often used to say I was fine to family members as I couldn't cope with them crying, and that was for two reasons. Firstly, I didn't want them to be in pain; but secondly, I felt so broken myself that having then to try to pick someone else up off the floor was something I simply couldn't handle, physically or mentally. The issue with all of the above is that it stops you being real about what you are going through. At some point, you have to draw a line and say, firstly, 'I can't protect others from the pain of loss, and, if I try to, I am actually robbing them of the chance to process their grief.' Secondly, people don't expect the grieving person to help them, so it is okay to stand back and say, 'It hurts, doesn't it?' This is then a time for you all to cry together, and not a time for you to become the superhero and save them from the grief.

TASK FOR THE DAY

Consider whether you are trying to rescue people from grief. Just as they can't save you from this pain, you can't rescue them either. Choose to be real in all circumstances, even if that means a friend or family member regularly sharing tears with you. Those who grieve together heal together.

* *

And then, one cloudy afternoon, I decided it was time.
It was time to lay down my sword. To stop fighting the
pain. To give up the relentless battle not to cry. I fully
submitted. I looked into the eyes of suffering and
declared, 'I can do this. I will not run from you, grief.
I will give you the space you deserve.' And that,
my friend, is when my healing began.

* * * * * * * * * * * ZOË CLARK-COATES * * * * * * * * * * *

DAY 44

Tears have a voice. Pain has a voice. How often do we refuse to let that voice be heard, though? We just silence it and refuse to give it a time to talk. We learn so much about ourselves and the experience we have walked through if we do give tears and pain space to communicate.

At times my tears screamed of physical agony; at other times they spoke of desperation, of heartbreak, of fear and of dread. Grief and loss are so utterly confusing. A million emotions and a trillion feelings, and all of them are connected to this tiny, five-letter word called grief.

TASK FOR THE DAY

Write in the tear shapes below some of the key things your tears are trying to communicate.

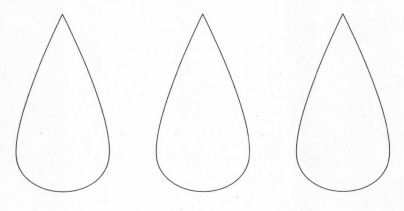

The world tells us it is good to be strong, it is great to be fearless. It feeds us messages that being broken is weakness and tears are self-indulgent. We are patted on the back if 'we held it together,' and are awarded a badge of bravery if we manage to fake a smile through the pain. I long for the day when as a community we say enough. Where we stand as one and say expressing human emotion is what makes us human. To show one's scars and to reveal hidden pain is heroic. Vulnerability is beautiful and once society embraces this we will give all people permission to be real . . . to be them.

ZOË CLARK-COATES

DAY 45

Impending loss.

One of the hardest things for me to live through was impending loss. It felt like my baby was hanging over a cliff edge and I was lying on the floor, clinging on to their hands for dear life. Time went so slowly; every day felt like a year and emotionally I was on a terrifying rollercoaster. One moment I was trying to believe everything would be okay, and the next second I was trying to prepare myself for the loss. I felt guilty for even considering they might not make it, and I felt ridiculous for daring to hope they might be okay. I dreaded going to the bathroom. I feared doing any activity in case that was the final straw and a loss then happened. The joy of pregnancy was stolen from me, and pregnancy felt like skydiving without a parachute. During this time, emotions adjust to being on high alert and adrenaline pumps through your veins 24/7. Post-loss, this doesn't simply cease, as your body has grown accustomed to living in what has felt like dangerous terrain, so as well as processing the grief, you also need to reprogramme your mind and let it learn to rest again, and allow for this fight-or-flight response to settle.

TASK FOR THE DAY

How do we reprogramme our mind and give it time to adjust if it has been in a state of high alert for some time? Firstly, talk, and keep talking so the brain can get to grips with the emotional turmoil you have had to process. Secondly, you need to find something to help you relax. This may be exercise, it may be relaxation therapy, it may be reading, but it needs to be something that lets your mind be calm and ideally gives you time off from thinking. We live in a world where stillness is hard to find; now is a time you need to seek it out and learn to stand still, breathe deeply and slow your heart rate. Try to do this today and every day going forwards.

* *

Some days it hurts from nowhere.

One moment the sun is shining through the window, which is making you smile, the next moment the grief consumes you like a tornado. It lifts you up and throws you into a heap of tears on the floor.

Grief is the ultimate force. A presence that needs no invite, it just enters the room whenever it pleases. This is why we need to respect it and to honour it.

It will journey with you now for life, and only you can choose whether it is the enemy or a reluctant companion.

* * * * * * * * * * * ZOË CLARK-COATES * * * * * * * * * *

DAY 46

My babies were robbed of all their tomorrows, but because of them I embrace all of my todays – and you can too. This isn't me saying look on the bright side; it's me purely saying that in all of this pain, in all of this brokenness, our children offer us beautiful gifts. And one of these gifts is an appreciation of life and a tangible sense of the fragility of life, which can make you seize every joy-filled moment with two hands. For a long time, I couldn't feel anything but pain, but, as time went on, I became aware of these beautiful gifts.

TASK FOR THE DAY

Do you feel in a place where you can see the gifts your baby(ies) brought you? If you do, list them below. If you can't see them as yet, list below the gifts you hope they will bring.

1 _____

2 _____

3 _____

4 _____

5 _____

6 _____

7 _____

* *

When my babies went ahead of me, their departure created a seismic hole in my life. I was acutely aware that I could let that space be filled with pain and horrific memories, or I could fill it with beauty and a lasting legacy to show the world that they lived. I chose the latter, as everyone, absolutely everyone, deserves to be remembered with a smile.

* * * * * * * * * * ZOË CLARK-COATES * * * * * * * * * *

DAY 47

If yesterday you ran from the pain . . . but today you sit with the pain . . . and tomorrow you face the pain . . . that, my friend, is the journey to healing a broken heart.

So please don't panic. Please don't feel you should be further along the path than you currently are.

You are doing fine. You don't need to walk at someone else's speed. You don't need to fret if people make you feel you are healing too slowly; that is their issue, not yours.

Your loss.

Your pain.

Your walk.

TASK FOR THE DAY

Write a letter to yourself pre-loss, giving yourself your best tips for how to navigate loss. Then look at that letter – are you now following your own advice?

Dear Me,

When you are bereft and you find someone who speaks the language of grief, it feels like 'home'.

ZOË CLARK-COATES

DAY 48

* *

Have you ever cried for so long you are scared? Scared you will never stop weeping? Scared that this is how life will look for ever? Scared that you will never smile again?

This fear is so normal and it is okay to acknowledge it, and it helps to discuss it.

When grief grips your soul, it feels bleak and desolate, and this lack of hope for a brighter tomorrow is part of the grieving process.

I promise you the sun will rise and this scary, black grief will lessen.

Try to not even consider what tomorrow has in store when you feel the terror take hold; just focus on today. If today seems too much to handle, just get through the next hour. Whether you take massive steps forwards, or the tiniest micro steps, it doesn't matter; progress is being made – and you, my friend, are going to make it through.

TASK FOR THE DAY

Write down in these steps the six things you can do to help you get through today:

- -

In the weeks and months I carried you, I knew what
a precious gift you were.

You were my fairy-tale ending. My bucket-list request.
My genie-in-the-bottle wish.

Not an hour went by that I did not appreciate your
presence in my world.

- - - - - - - - - - ZOË CLARK-COATES - - - - - - - - - - -

DAY 49

Broken hearts continue to beat.

Now I see this as a good thing, but when I was broken it was the last thing I wanted to hear. I didn't want my heart to carry on beating, I wanted to be saved from the pain. So if that's how you feel today, I want you to know that I get it, I hear your pain.

There is a phrase commonly bandied about that I used to hate with a passion, and that is: 'time heals all wounds'. Is it correct? No, time doesn't automatically heal all wounds, but it is possible for the wounds to no longer bleed. And, yes, that does happen over time and can't be fast-forwarded. So, while I wish I could point you in the direction of a secret trap door that fast-forwards time for you, I sadly can't, and I just hope you can believe me when I say this . . .

It will get easier.

You are going to make it through this black tunnel.

Just hold on.

TASK FOR THE DAY

Find something to distract you for 15 minutes today. It could be listening to a piece of music you adore that has lots of happy memories attached to it, or losing yourself in a good movie. You can think of anything but loss and pain – this is your 15 minutes to escape.

* *

Not everyone stays for ever. Some people arrive, change us and then leave. How we continue on once they have departed is what shows the world they were ever here at all.

* * * * * * * * * * ZOË CLARK-COATES * * * * * * * * * * *

DAY 50

Oh, how I wish the world would recognise and acknowledge that one person can never replace another. Also, grieving in no way shows a lack of gratitude for another living soul. Pain and joy, tears and smiles, even regret and thankfulness can easily sit alongside one another, so don't let anyone tell you any different, my friend.

You can feel it all . . . In the same hour you can scream and laugh. You can feel helpless and hopeful. You can want to die and want to live. You can want to have more children, and never want to have another.

This is what grieving looks like: a consortium of opposing feelings in one mind, in one body. You are normal to feel it all.

TASK FOR THE DAY

How would you describe your grief today?

* *

If you start questioning, 'Why me?', you can end up
feeling like a victim. Flipping that question on its
head and saying, 'Why not me?' can help you rise
to the battle at hand.

ZOË CLARK-COATES

DAY 51

Baby loss is made up of 'if only's. If only I held you. If only I raised you. If only I knew what your personality would have been like.

I used to constantly ask myself how, as a parent, do I console myself, knowing the millions of questions I have will never be answered? I thought I was destined to live in turmoil and internal conflict, but I was wrong. I found peace with not knowing. That doesn't mean I still wouldn't love to know all the answers; it just means I learnt to accept that I can't know.

There wasn't a magical moment when this peace arrived, and it wasn't something I did that made it happen. Over time I just gradually became accustomed to living with the unknowns, and that brought with it a feeling of being okay to live with a million question marks.

I hope one day you too find some peace in the not knowing.

TASK FOR THE DAY

In what areas of your life would you like to feel more peace?

[blank lined box]

Is there anything you can do to get that peace? If there is, consider doing it . . .

* *

Your story. Your pain. Your loss. All of it, every single part of it, deserves to be heard. Deserves to be recognised. Deserves to be given time to heal.

* * * * * * * * * * * ZOË CLARK-COATES * * * * * * * * * *

DAY 52

When we are young, we are taught how to articulate joy and happiness but we are rarely taught the language of loss. How does one even begin to express earth-shattering pain? Loss flings you into a world of medical terminology, and while trying to translate that you are simultaneously expected to explain to those around you the depth of heartache you are experiencing. I just wanted people to understand that my world was unravelling in front of my eyes, and however much I begged for the pain to stop, it didn't. But I couldn't find the words in my fog of grief to tell them anything other than, 'I am hurting.'

TASK FOR THE DAY

What are you struggling to express to those around you?
Use this space to try to verbalise what you would want the
world to know.

* *

Just because someone isn't publicly weeping, doesn't
mean their heart isn't privately breaking.

* * * * * * * * * * ZOË CLARK-COATES * * * * * * * * * *

DAY 53

My soul seemed to know what to do to survive . . . it wanted to talk, to explain, to express, to verbalise the agony my heart was trying to process. My mind on the other hand wanted me to be silent, to not risk more pain – to share means to be vulnerable, and when you reveal heartache you have suffered, you in turn invite comments from those who hear your story. So the mission is to be guided by your soul, whilst quietening your thoughts, so your heart can start to mend.

I looked for people who inspired me to step out . . . I needed to be encouraged to voice my story and I encourage you to do the same.

TASK FOR THE DAY

Who inspires you and why? Even by considering this question you are looking beyond the superficial and looking deep. The people we often admire and respect don't have it all together; they are the people who are real about life.

* *

When you fear you can't handle another day on this planet, just remind yourself you can and you will. Your heart can't even comprehend the hidden strength your mind holds.

* * * * * * * * * * * ZOË CLARK-COATES * * * * * * * * * *

DAY 54

Every once in a while, we discover a person who changes our perspective on life. They fearlessly and perhaps even without knowing it guide us on our personal journey. They make us smile, but will just as happily sit with us as we shed a million tears. These people are sacred, and we won't meet many of them on our walk through life, so cherish them, hold them close and treat them with love, as they will be a lamp in the darkness.

TASK FOR THE DAY

Friends and family can transform our experience of loss, and take it from being one of isolation to one filled with love. Who are the friends who have helped you survive your journey of loss? Has any friend surprised you with their kindness?

Friends Who Have Helped Me

***

Only I knew of your existence . . . and only I was aware of your departure.

ZOË CLARK-COATES

DAY 55

What makes people tired when they are grieving? Is it the lack of hope that makes them so weary? Is it the immense pain they are carrying in their heart that weighs them down? Is it the dread of a new day bringing another 24 hours for them to face? Is it that grief robs them of deep and restful sleep as they are haunted by nightmares of loss?

Whatever it is, grief is utterly exhausting. If you feel spent, broken, tired and don't know how you can even face today, trust me when I say your energy will return. My advice is to be selective in terms of what you choose to do, and use the energy you do have for basic survival, until strength returns to you.

TASK FOR THE DAY

Rest. This is your task. True rest if that is possible. Take a long shower, or lie in the bath and relax. Thirty minutes of doing nothing.

What do you love to do, but never have time for? Think how you can make time in your life to do this more.

I was so tired.

My heart was tired.

My brain was tired.

My tears were tired.

I begged to feel numb, so numb
I could sleep without nightmares.

Just 24 hours without feeling crippling pain in my heart.

But grief doesn't give you time off. Not a day, not
an hour, not even a crummy minute.

Grief doesn't care if you are tired.

Grief just wants to be felt.

Grief just wants to be heard.

This is why grieving is exhausting,
as there is no respite.

ZOË CLARK-COATES

DAY 56

What do you wish you had known about grief before experiencing it?

There are so many things I wished I had known. Firstly, I wish I had been aware that grief consumes you, every part of you, and it makes you feel lost and alone, but this feeling does pass. I was so scared when this happened to me, and if I had known the feelings wouldn't last for ever that would have really helped me.

I wish I had known that I am not responsible for others' grief. I felt so guilty that our losses brought so much pain to other people's lives, so I tried to rescue them from that. I now wish I had just let them process their pain and not used my small energy reserves to protect them.

I wish I had known it was okay to smile, and by me smiling I wasn't in any way saying my babies' lives didn't matter. The fear of this held me back from laughing for so long.

TASK FOR THE DAY

What do you wish you had known?

1 _____

2 _____

3 _____

4 _____

5 _____

* *

If only loving someone meant they were guaranteed
to stay, how much sweeter would life be.

* * * * * * * * * * ZOË CLARK-COATES * * * * * * * * * *

DAY 57

We are taught that grief has neat steps – I can almost laugh at that now. Oh, how simple it would be if we could have a tick list of grief stepping stones, where we carefully leap from one step to the next.

Grief isn't like that. This is what grief looks like:

What people think the journey of grief looks like . . .

What it actually looks like

When we can accept that grief isn't linear, I think it truly helps our journey through loss, as most grieving people fear they have lost the plot. All their emotions have gone haywire and they have no clue what they will feel like minute by minute.

So, trust me when I say grief isn't neat; it's messy and it is hard and whether you are standing today, or lying on the floor weeping, you are doing fine.

TASK FOR THE DAY

Draw a picture of what your grief looks like:

People spend so much time trying to get back to who
they were pre-loss, and even if they got there (which they
can't) they would discover they no longer belong in that
world. The space they left is no longer their shape. The
only way to find the new them is to move forwards.

ZOË CLARK-COATES

DAY 58

Surviving baby loss is like swimming in the ocean with no clue as to whether you can swim. You don't enter the water at the shore, you get dropped into the deepest part, and no land is even in sight. Waves often go over your head and you are convinced you will drown.

Then you see a lifebuoy and reach out to it, knowing it is your one chance of survival. You grab it with a very weak hand, and cling to it for dear life.

Only when strength has returned can you attempt to swim again. With fear and trepidation, you decide to attempt to reach dry land, and launch into the waves. As you discover you can in fact swim, you look to your left and then to your right, and that is when you see a host of other people swimming in the same direction.

You are not alone. Everyone has the same look of fear on their face, but together you are stronger. As one, you swim to land.

And that, my friend, is how you survive baby loss . . . Together. In unity. All terrified. All unsure whether you can swim. All afraid of the water.

But the strength of swimming in the same direction carries you through to land.

TASK FOR THE DAY

Find a piece of music that encourages you and makes you feel you do have the strength to make it to land.

One of my favourite songs which spurs me on is Whitney Houston's 'I Did Not Know My Own Strength'!

* *

Oh, how I used to wish that I didn't feel everything so intensely. I longed to be a person who just experienced things at a superficial level, where a simple sweep of the hand would banish any hurt I felt.

But I wasn't that person. I felt it all. Deeply. Crushingly. The pain was ceaseless. The grief was unyielding.

I had assumed that was my great weakness but I couldn't have been more wrong, as this was actually my superpower.

Because I felt it all, I had no choice but to embrace it, to process it, and to allow it to change me. Through the pain, I discovered who I was, and by holding on to hope I found my purpose.

* * * * * * * * * * * ZOË CLARK-COATES * * * * * * * * * * *

DAY 59

So many lose babies when they have never even told a single person they are pregnant. It is so hard to tell people you have lost if they didn't even know you were pregnant. I so wish I could rewind the clock and be more open about all of my pregnancies, as talking would then have been so much easier.

One of the key campaigns of the Mariposa Trust (sayinggoodbye.org) is to break the '12-week rule', which advocates not telling people you are pregnant until after 12 weeks of pregnancy, just in case you lose the baby. This is a blatant message not to talk about loss. We need to fight this, and speak of our precious children from the moment we feel ready to share the news.

TASK FOR THE DAY

What other hidden or subtle messages do you feel the world or those around you are trying to impose on you?

While you remember them,
they will live for ever.

ZOË CLARK-COATES

DAY 60

* *

I often wonder, when do friends become family? It is certainly not dictated by the length of the relationship, as some friends come into your life and within hours they are family. So what is it? Where, how and when does this magic happen? I believe it happens when your souls connect. Within minutes of the conversation starting, you can tell you are on the same wavelength. You feel instantly comfortable with sharing intimate truths and revealing hidden parts of your heart. You know they would be your 3am call should crisis strike, and your gut tells you that they would never ask, 'Why are you calling?'; they would just say, 'How can I help?' Forever friends . . . that is what they are called.

TASK FOR THE DAY

Who are your forever friends?

Are there others you feel you could become closer to? If yes, what could you do to make those relationships stronger?

```



```

* *

Free yourself from wrong expectation.

There is no fixed time period in which the darkest part of grief must pass. There isn't a timeframe in which you must smile or even function. There is no worldly standard for what is 'normal' when it comes to mourning a loved one. This is a myth spun by those who don't know how grief works – those lucky souls who have never been on the receiving end of a life-changing loss.

So, however you feel today – that is normal.

However much you hurt – that is normal.

How much you cry – that is normal.

Your grief.

Your loss.

Your normal.

* * * * * * * * * * *   ZOË CLARK-COATES   * * * * * * * * * * *

Help and Resources

International Support Following Baby Loss

Advice, support, befriending, international remembrance services, counselling, support via social media and more.

The Mariposa Trust – Saying Goodbye is the primary division which offers support post-baby loss, but the charity has many other divisions too.
* mariposatrust.org
* sayinggoodbye.org

Marriage Counselling and Support

* relate.org.uk
* themarriagecourses.org/try/the-marriage-course/

Support for Children Who Are Grieving

* winstonswish.org
* youngminds.org.uk

Twins and Multiple Births

* tamba.org.uk
* sparks.org.uk/our-research/

Genetic Support

* contact.org.uk
* mencap.org.uk
* soft.org.uk
* kleefstrasyndrome.org
* downs-syndrome.org.uk
* williams-syndrome.org.uk
* tss.org.uk
* hda.org.uk
* rettuk.org
* geneticdisordersuk.org/partnershipnetwork/members

Bereavement Support and Counselling

* mariposatrust.org
* soultears.org
* sayinggoodbye.org
* psychotherapy.org.uk/find-a-therapist/
* cruse.org.uk
* childbereavementuk.org
* mind.org.uk
* nhs.uk/conditions/counselling/
* bacp.co.uk/search/Therapists
* acc-uk.org
* anxietyuk.org.uk
* counselling-directory.org.uk
* mindandsoulfoundation.org

Emotional Support for People in Distress

* Samaritans – samaritans.org
* SOBS – uksobs.org

Adoption

* adoptionuk.org
* gov.uk/child-adoption
* homeforgood.org.uk
* afteradoption.org.uk

Fertility Charity Support

* fertilitynetworkuk.org

Pre- and Post-natal Depression

* pandasfoundation.org.uk
* tommys.org/pregnancy-information/im-pregnant/mental-wellbeing/specific-mental-health-conditions/postnatal-depression
* nct.org.uk/life-parent/how-you-might-be-feeling/postnatal-depression-questions-you-really-want-ask

Other Useful Contacts

* bereavementadvice.org
* nhs.uk
* mayoclinic.org

Thank You

Firstly, I want to thank you for choosing to read this book. I know it takes a lot to trust someone enough to let them in when you are grieving, and the fact you are reading my words means so much.

Huge thanks to all the families who kindly shared their stories for this book, in the hope it makes others feel less alone. Emily Gray, Ashely Vaughan, Rebecca Rickman-Jenkins, Lauren Burton, Sarah Clarke, Jo Hart, Gio Cook, Chris Cook, Laura White, Andy White, Jen, Lauren Riboldi, Caitlin Turner, Catherine Clark, Sarah Henderson, Nick Henderson, Nicole Bowles, Jennie McFerran, Matthew McFerran, Jessica Smallwood, Martin Leggatt, Susi Leggatt, Claire Fitchie, Heidi, Jane, Cassie Smith, Rachel Moss, Amy Haguma, Helen Fosberry, Esther Vaughan, Anya, Sarah Macdonald, Emily Cooke, Janey Lewins, Amie Devers, Katy Kear, Andrew Stanton and Siobhan Abrahams. For some of you, I know it was the first time you have shared your stories, for others you share it regularly – I am so very grateful that you trusted me and my book to voice your words.

Thanks to Professor Kathryn Gutteridge for her contribution. Kathryn, you are a wonderful midwife, mother and grandmother who knows the pain of loss first-hand. Thank you for supporting me, this book and the work of our charity internationally.

Thanks to Anya Sizer for her contribution. Anya, you are not only a fertility expert and campaigner for change, you are also my good friend. Thank you for being willing to share your fertility expertise within these pages.

Thanks to my agent Jane Maw and my editor Olivia Morris and Amanda Harris, and all who have helped make this book come to pass at Orion Spring/Hachette. You believe in me and my work and a mere thank you doesn't seem sufficient, to be honest, but thank you – thank you for entrusting me with and for giving me this platform to write books and support more people.

Thanks to the team at the Mariposa Trust: all of you have cheered me on while I was writing this book, and I am so grateful to each of you. The charity team are not just 'team', they are so much more than that; they are family. Each of you are my heroes, you give up so much of your time and dedicate so much of your life to helping others and it is only by us working together globally that we are able to support as many people as we do.

Thank you to my wonderful friends who have supported me while writing this. I am not going to list you all, but you know who you are . . .

Thanks to my parents, who not only read each chapter as I wrote it, but also encouraged me every step of the way. I love you both and feel blessed to have you as not only my parents, but some of my best friends.

Thanks to my sister Hayley, brother-in-law Justin, nieces Aimee and Carys and nephew Joshua. You are not just family you are some of my closest friends and it is an honour to do life with you. Hayley – we have lived through everything together, you are my witness in life – we have been children together, grandchildren together, and are now mothers together. To have another person on the planet who says word for word the same thing as me at exactly the same time is pretty special; I am so glad God gave me you as a sister.

Thanks to my grandad for supporting and loving me. Oh, how I wish Nan had lived to see my first book published and now this second book. The endless love you both displayed right till the end of her life gave me an even greater understanding of grief – so thank you for being so authentic in your sorrow.

And now a MASSIVE, GIGANTIC thank you to Andy and my two daughters, Esme Emilia and Bronte Jemima.

Andy, you are always in my corner cheering me on, empowering me and encouraging me. You have personally created the time and space for me to even have the chance to put pen to paper; without you doing that, this book wouldn't even exist, so THANK YOU. You have read every word I have written a hundred times, and whenever I have doubted myself you have whispered in my ear, 'This is amazing, keep on going.' You are my soulmate, my bestest friend and the love of my entire life. Thank you for being every kind of wonderful. I adore you and I will love you for ever.

To my girls, Esme Emilia Promise and Bronte Jemima Hope. Firstly, thank you for allowing me the time and space to write this book. Whenever I have said, 'Mummy needs to write now', you have always happily let me do it, and have constantly told me how proud you are that I write to help people with broken hearts. You are both beautiful miracles, who I longed for, prayed for and celebrate every single day. To say I am proud of who you are and the characters you constantly display is an understatement; you are both world-changers, light bringers, and I am honoured to be your mum. I love you both to the moon and back . . . and back again.

Legacy Scheme

If this book has helped you, would you consider purchasing copies to help others?

Maybe you would like to buy a couple of copies for friends or family who have lost, or perhaps you might like to purchase copies in bulk? Many people around the world have fundraised to enable them to buy hundreds of copies of my first book, *Saying Goodbye*, in honour of the baby they have lost. They then donate these books to hospitals, clinics, GP practices, churches or support groups, so anyone who has lost a baby gets given a copy as soon as they have encountered loss. They even write a personal message to the bereaved family in each book.

I would love people to do this with *The Baby Loss Guide*.

Maybe you feel you would like to be part of supporting others through grief and perhaps you could consider doing this?

For more information, email:
legacy@thebabylossguide.org

About the Author

Zoë Clark-Coates BCAh is an award-winning charity CEO, business leader, counsellor, conference speaker, journalist, author and TV show host. For over 20 years she has been a trailblazer within PR, events and the media.

Following the loss of five babies, she co-founded the charity the Mariposa Trust (widely known by the name of its primary division, sayinggoodbye.org) with her husband Andy, enabling her to use her training as a counsellor on a daily basis.

As an innovative leader, she has steered the charity to become a leading support organisation in the UK and globally, providing support that reaches over 50,000 people each week.

As a gifted communicator, she has earned the respect of politicians, the government and many high-profile celebrities and influencers. Zoë's skill as a writer prompted Arianna Huffington to invite her to start writing for the *Huffington Post*, which created the perfect platform to reach a new audience.

She has her own TV talk show called *Soul Tears*, where she interviews celebrities and people of note about their journeys through loss. She is also a trusted expert and media commentator for many other programmes on the BBC, ITV and Channel 5.

Zoë was appointed by the Secretary of State for Health as co-chair of the National Pregnancy Loss Review. As co-chair, she is responsible for advising the government and Department of Health on how better support and clinical care can be offered.